Seizing Our Destiny

2012's best communities to live, work, grow and prosper in – and how they got that way

By Robert Bell, John Jung & Louis Zacharilla

With a Foreword by Suvi Linden, Commissioner, UN Commission for Digital Development

Published by the
Intelligent Community Forum
www.intelligentcommunity.org

© 2012 Intelligent Community Forum All rights reserved.

First edition, published by Intelligent Community Forum
250 Park Avenue, 7th Floor, New York, NY 10177 USA
+1 646-291-6166, fax +1 212-825-0075 www.intelligentcommunity.org

Table of Contents

Foreword	7
All Life is Local	15
Why Seven?	19
Austin, Texas USA *A tale of two economies*	23
What Innovation Means – And What It Doesn't	33
Oulu, Finland *Riding the waves of change*	39
How Intelligent Communities Create Innovation Ecosystems	47
Quebec City, Quebec, Canada *Turning a provincial capital into a magnet for talent*	53
How They Seized Their Destiny	63
Riverside, California, USA *Creating an innovation ecosystem from scratch*	69
Lessons from Intelligent Communities	83
Saint John, New Brunswick, Canada *A city in distress builds a collaborative future*	87
More Lessons from Intelligent Communities	99
Stratford, Ontario, Canada *Leveraging a history of reinvention*	107
More Lessons from Intelligent Communities	121
Taichung City, Taiwan *A Mechanical Kingdom leads in the digital age*	129
The Path Forward	139
Appendix	145

Intelligent Community Forum

Shoutout

This publication is made possible by the contributions of many people and institutions around the world. ICF would especially like to acknowledge the "Friends of the Forum."

Without their support, both financial and intellectual, the Intelligent Community movement could not spread its ideas and tell these stories of risk, perseverance and success. It would be impossible as well for us to sustain the level of "emotional transportation" which allows us to pass along stories of communities that are transforming human society and bringing hope everywhere. Thanks to these companies, people and organizations, along with many others whose names we cannot record here, our voice remains present and unique as our global dialogue continues to influence the future of cities, regions and towns.

A special acknowledgement goes to the following organizations, whose financial support enabled the publication of *Seizing Our Destiny*:

- **Bell**
- **BusinessOulu**
- **Enterprise Saint John**
- **FIABCI-Chinese Taiwan**
- **The Herbert W. Hoover Foundation**
- **The Institute for the Study of the Intelligent Community at Walsh University**
- **The Lee Ming Construction Company**

- **Motorola Solutions**
- **Oulun Energia**
- **Riverside Public Utilities**
- **The Riverside Unified School District**
- **The City of Stratford**
- **Xerox**
- **Vee TIME Corp.**

Special acknowledgement also goes to Professors Don Flournoy, Sylvie Albert and Tomoko Kanayama, and to Jagadish ("Jag") Rao, Ann Kayman, Professor Mel Horwitch of Central European University, Jerry Hultin and the Polytechnic Institute of New York University, all of whom have been instrumental partners in bringing the world's best communities forward for others to see.

ICF thanks its selection jury, made up of citizens from all walks of life around the globe. These men and woman on every continent spend precious time each year to ensure that the Top7 receive a fair hearing as they pursue the Intelligent Community of the Year honor.

Finally, we acknowledge the civic leaders and citizens of the Top7 Intelligent Communities of 2012. Without their dedication, courage and bold pursuit of ideas for rebuilding communities, we would have no stories to tell.

In 2012, one of the Top7 – Riverside, California, USA – was named Intelligent Community of the Year. ICF takes the title of this book from the name that Riverside gave to its 2009 community vision and roadmap, which spurred such a powerful transformation. A community's destiny is indeed in the hands of those with the heads and the hearts to seize it.

Robert Bell, John Jung, Louis Zacharilla
Founders, Intelligent Community Forum

Foreword

■ SUVI LINDEN, COMMISSIONER,
UNITED NATIONS COMMISSION FOR DIGITAL DEVELOPMENT

By the end of the decade, development in communications and information technology will make the world a very different place, one based on a fully digital economy. Telecommunication networks offer a chance and hope for economic growth in even the poorest countries in which the future did not previously appear very bright. The Millennium Goals set by the United Nations are receiving a new boost through the use of broadband. With the right leadership, much faster development is possible than could have been dreamt of even a few years ago. Among the reasons is the recognition of the possibilities by local governments and communities worldwide, which sense a new paradigm emerging.

Mobile and fiber optic networks are being bu ilt all over the globe in developed and emerging countries. Three-quarters of the world's population now has access to and can use a mobile phone. The real power of broadband lies in its potential to improve development outcomes around the world.

Mobile communications – and more specifically, mobile broadband – now offer significant opportunities to advance socio-economic development. Studies show that ten percent growth in broadband penetration adds one to three percent to a country's gross domestic product. Over three million banking customers are now using mobile phones in

Kenya, a huge success story; people can make cash payments and set aside valuable savings using mobile phones.

The vital issue is to make broadband available and affordable. A need now exists for visionary governments, who understand that the power of telecom infrastructure is as important as traditional transport routes and that the digital economy is the key to a better life for citizens. Solutions should be found locally for the effective use of ICT, in order to provide a better, more intelligent environment for citizens.

Cultural awareness is not always connected to the high-tech world of ICT. Yet, increasingly, digital technologies play an important role in this rather "intangible economy," as they provide new forms of social interaction and contribute significantly to new expressions of creativity. Cultural awareness also helps us to understand each other better. By exchanging information on different habits around the world, we can create new ways of thinking and doing things. Music and different forms of art provide us with excellent ways to express our identity and our deepest values and share them around the world. As the former Minister of Culture and Minister of Communications for my nation, I know how much the arts teach people: how to create, inspire imagination and believe in their own potential.

ICT and access to information can enhance innovation by first allowing an understanding of different values and ways of thinking from different parts of the world. New innovations are often created by challenging old habits and by seeing traditional processes from a new angle. There is always more to learn about ourselves. ICT can, remarkably, enhance our understanding of each other. We should take every opportunity to promote equality between different people in different parts of the world. We have the tools, and they are becoming increasingly available. We also have organizations, and one in particular, which has dedicated itself to conducting a global dialogue on this aspect of technology and community.

The Intelligent Community Forum (ICF) works within this crucially important area, and asks daily how technology can be used to create both individual and collective intelligence. The five themes or indicators of the ICF's philosophy – infrastructure, innovation, the knowledge workforce, digital inclusion, and advocacy and marketing – build an excellent framework for communities to develop inclusive prosperity on a foundation of information and communications technology.

The Intelligent Community of the Year Award Program has given hundreds of communities a platform to analyze how information and communication technology have been implemented in their societies. Citizens can enjoy the benefits, including the generation of new innovations. Participation in the award program offers an ideal opportunity to learn. The application requires that an applicant city or community become profoundly absorbed in the theme at hand. The program is unique because it is suitable for both big and small cities, as well as both rural and urban communities and regions. It is not about location; it is, as ICF says, about our civil destinies.

An opportunity to study the work carried out in the Top7 communities is vitally useful. All of the Top7 communities have a distinct and effective vision and strategy, and each is a place that can be benchmarked thanks to the program, and which employ compelling technology and information design that is for intergenerational longevity.

As the digital economy evolves, partnerships are becoming increasingly commonplace and essential. The ICF provides a network in which communities can exchange best practices, learn from each other, and benchmark experiences. All communities have a common interest in using ICT efficiently and in innovative ways. Partnership in a network makes it possible to overcome obstacles or avoid them by learning from other members, offering an excellent showroom for public e-services. The private sector can find partners and business opportunities through involvement in a community.

Technology is ubiquitous in my home city of Oulu, Finland, which is a pioneer in the development of many new technologies, particularly mobile networks and devices. Partnerships between Oulu's public and private sector have been extensive, and the city has built an innovative environment for ICT development. Involvement in the Intelligent Community Award Program enhanced Oulu's confidence and taught us detailed lessons about the challenges of marketing and advocacy. I believe the city should be more active in communicating with its citizens, and that we should address the challenges in advocating our track record for businesses and in attracting new investment to the region. Oulu can use the findings of the Intelligent Community Award Program and its partnership in ICF's network of thought leaders and its Foundation to help build a digital roadmap for the city.

I have personally worked as a politician at both local and national level. It has always been important to me to consider how to improve the quality of the living environment for citizens. I believe that within the mandate to improve living conditions there are not only many business opportunities for companies, but as we see in Oulu and other Intelligent Communities among the Top7, the chance to create new industries as well.

Fifty percent of productivity growth in the private sector is due to ICT. The current global economic crisis and low productivity in public sector services should accelerate the use of ICT, e-services and mobile applications. Attracting citizens to use new applications and services is a challenge; using ICT also demands a new way of doing things. Many current processes must be reformed, which is often difficult and complicated. Implementing new technological innovations into daily routines is tough, and may be the reason for low productivity in the public sector. Pilot projects too often remain pilot projects. However, as this year's Top7 demonstrated to an eager global audience while in New York, concept has been put into action in a very significant way.

The Broadband Commission of ITU and UNESCO has set as a target that every country in the world should have a national broadband strategy by the end of year 2015 for shaping future social and economic development. The five cornerstones of the ICF's philosophy offer a framework for creating a community's digital strategy. The challenge is to enhance those five sectors and to ensure that they are in balance with each other. Every community, large or small, should create its own roadmap for the digital world ahead of us, and a strategy that evaluates the impact of ICT and reflects the philosophy of the ICF.

I have found it so very rewarding to be part of the Intelligent Community movement, launched by ICF several years ago. I warmly recommend communities to take part in the Intelligent Community Award Program. Understanding the philosophy of the ICF offers a solid platform to strengthen the competitiveness and success of any community. Is not that what we really want and need for our children?

The world is changing quickly – and the ecosystem around our living environments changes rapidly due to global trends. We all know that speed of response matters. The vitality of a region or community can be measured by its elasticity and capacity for quick adjustments. ICF promotes tools for communities to maintain and enhance regional vitality.

The Top7 Intelligent Communities of 2012, which you will read about in this volume, were led by Riverside, California, which emerged as the Intelligent Community of the Year. Each has a story of success to share. Each is alike in that it seized its destiny, especially during harsh times, and succeeded while maintaining its sense of identity and culture. Each has made its region more vital. I commend them and their stories to you.

Suvi Linden is the former Minister of Communications and Minister of Culture, Finland, a former member of Finland's National Parliament and currently a member of Council in her home city, Oulu. In 2011, ICF named her its Intelligent Community Visionary of the Year.

The Top7 Intelligent Communities of 2012

All Life is Local

■ ROBERT BELL, CO-FOUNDER, ICF

Whether you live in a small town or great city, you live your life at the local level. Whether your passport is filled with immigration stamps or you see no need for a passport, you live in a particular place of your birth or of your choosing.

The community is where you are born and where you will die. It is where your children are educated (or not), your basic needs are met (or not), and the small concerns and high dramas of your life unfold. That place has a name and, to a greater or lesser extent, it has named you. And if you are lucky, it is a place you value and that makes you feel valued in return.

As important as your community may be, however, it is just a small dot on a very large map. Its economy, culture and ways of life are intimately interwoven with those of other places: the capitals of nations, the centers of global finance, and the research and development hubs where tomorrow's breakthroughs are taking shape.

In the 21st Century, the world is very much at your doorstep. Because of accelerating advances in information and communications technology (ICT), the global economy is coming to dominate the life of the local community. It literally throws you into competition with people of similar talents and experience all around the planet. If your community cannot offer the right mix of skills, costs, quality infrastructure and access to markets, its economy will suffer, because ICT frees employers to shop the world for the best deal. And the "right mix" is not something fixed and immutable – it constantly evolves as poor nations become rich, tastes change and technology upends old assumptions.

But this storm cloud also has a silver lining. The same ICT revolution that threatens long-established ways of life also offers communities powerful new tools to build a better future. Communities large and small, in industrialized and developing nations, are finding ways to create prosperity, solve social challenges and strengthen their cultures on a foundation of ICT innovation. Rather than letting the global economy run roughshod, they are seizing their destinies with both hands and turning legacy into opportunity.

These are the communities that the Intelligent Community Forum studies.

Since 1999, the Forum has presented awards to honor communities for building and maintaining competitive and inclusive local economies in our ICT-driven global economy. We do it for two reasons. The first is to recognize amazing achievement by a group of global leaders. The second is to learn from them. To qualify for an award, communities share detailed information with us on how they did what they have done. We turn it into lessons for communities everywhere in need of help.

To be designated one of the Top7 Intelligent Communities – or even better, the Intelligent Community of the Year – nominees pass through an intensive analysis of their strategies, programs and results. We analyze them in five categories: broadband deployment, the ability to create and sustain a knowledge-based workforce, digital inclusion, innovation, marketing and advocacy. We call these our Intelligent Community Indicators (see page 145), the first framework for understanding how communities and regions can build sustainable, inclusive prosperity in today's "broadband economy."

In addition to the five Indicators, each annual Awards program includes a theme. In 2012, our theme was "Intelligent Communities: Platforms for Innovation." Innovation in Intelligent Communities brings together business, government and institutions in a dynamic partnership that produces results ranging from better and cheaper service delivery to citizens to the birth and growth of entrepreneurial businesses and vital new institutions. Intelligent Communities are pioneers in the complex collaboration that powers innovation today and are experts at building an innovation culture that attracts talent, investment and global recognition. By becoming platforms for innovation, Intelligent Communities create a better life for citizens on all rungs of the economic ladder and a vibrant future for the next generation.

How ICF Selects Intelligent Communities

It takes 12 months to find the Intelligent Community of the Year. In the first phase, ICF develops nominations for candidates from its own research and information submitted by communities using a simple, 6-question form. The nominations are reviewed by an ICF committee that scores each community on the six criteria of the Awards process.

We name the top-scoring group as our Smart21 Communities of the Year. Then we ask them to complete the far more detailed Top7 questionnaire. The completed questionnaires are read by a team of academic Analysts. The Analysts score the nominations based on performance against the Awards criteria, and we name the seven top-scoring candidates as ICF's Top7 Intelligent Communities.

In the final stage of the process, an independent research firm engaged by ICF re-analyzes the same data to produce a new set of scores. At the same time, ICF executives visit each of the Top7 and write reports, which are reviewed along with the nomination data by an international jury. The jury ranks the Top7, and ICF combines the two scores on a weighted basis to select the Intelligent Community of the Year.

In the following pages, you will meet the Top7 Intelligent Communities of 2012, including the one that became Intelligent Community of the Year. You will also learn more about how communities – including your own – can become platforms for innovation that creates prosperity and improves the quality of life for every citizen. ∎

Why Seven?

■ LOUIS ZACHARILLA, CO-FOUNDER, ICF

Wherever I go, I am asked two questions regarding the Intelligent Community of the Year Awards. The first is: "Why seven communities?" Why not pick ten or a more symmetrical number like 12? The second question asks how we select a "winner" from such a group of diverse, profoundly successful communities.

My first response is to joke that lists of ten or more have been taken, most famously in the United States by David Letterman and his Late Show TV program. However, when creating the Top7 awards program in 2002, I discovered that the number seven is, like the communities in the Top7 list, persistent. In fact, human beings may persistently use the number seven to make more lists than any other. Think of it: in Western culture there are Seven Deadly Sins; Seven Wonders of the World; and Seven Liberal Arts. Those interested in philosophy know that there were seven sages of ancient Greece and, in later Christianity, Seven Virtues (no doubt to balance those Seven Deadly Sins!). In our modern era, with its obsessive focus on technology, efficiency and multi-tasking, we know that highly effective people have seven habits! We all seek that, do we not? But efficiency and effectiveness are not modern inventions born in Riverside, Suwon or Stockholm. In one famous account, we read that it took seven days to make the entire universe.

(Well, actually it took six. On the seventh day the job which started all jobs was done, and the boss rested.)

The world has added many more lists of seven since the Big Bang. Now there are Seven Wonders of the Industrial World. For those of us who like the ocean, there are now Seven Wonders of the Underwater World and, in true American style, USA Today reported in 2006 that there are now seven new and improved (as they say in the advertising business) Wonders of the World.

Old or new, intelligent lists of seven are found everywhere. My personal favorite remains Gandhi's "Seven Blunders of the World." The Mahatma's list is the one worth repeating:

1. Wealth without work
2. Pleasure without conscience
3. Knowledge without character
4. Commerce without morality
5. Science without morality
6. Worship without sacrifice
7. Politics without principle

This list has inspired me because it articulates the code of conduct by which Intelligent Communities thrive. It also serves as their warning flag. Each community in the Top7 is mindful of the need to build community with a conscience, and that is what makes the Top7 special.

Intelligent Communities, especially the Top7, have become global symbols and are widely admired. They are increasingly teachers and, like all mentors, widely imitated. The ICF method of "emotional transportation," which is the way of story-telling and sharing best practices which remains at the heart of the movement, requires that we embrace technology, but never for its own sake. Technologies like broadband are applied within the evolving texture of real human community which, increasingly, relies upon collaboration and rediscovered "tribalism." When fused with an enlightened, universal idea like Gandhi's mandate, our worried sense of shrinking spaces and lost places in a world burgeoning with people, pursuing wealth and quality of life in numbers never before imagined, can be accommodated. As this occurs, and it is being done more than ever community by community, we can – dare we think it! –live more peacefully in any place we chose to call "home."

A final, inspiring list of seven is found in another corner of the Hindu world: the wedding tradition. The Sevenfold Vows symbolize the beginning of a bride and groom's new journey. The third and the seventh vows are relevant to our work because the third one declares that, "Together we shall share each other's ideals." As we follow the Top7 and build sustainable and wholesome communities everywhere – a common set of criteria and ideals keep us focused. The seventh vow concludes with the uncomfortable truth of our time. But it is a truth that can also inspire us and it does.

"Together we will look toward the uncertainties of the future with awe, open-mindedness and inspiration."

Many cultures believe that seven is a lucky number. Before the year's Top7 set out on their long journey, which they hope will end on a stage in New York bathed in applause as they are each referred to as "one of the world's Top7 Intelligent Communities," they hope for the best. It is not an easy path. Yet like newlyweds, they bring together many in their community – many for the first time. They then go through the process to complete the nomination form and to begin a 10-month journey of self-discovery. If they are lucky, but especially if they are good, they are invited to New York for the honeymoon.

How do we pick a "winner" from a group like this? We do not. We declare them all winners and get on with the important work of making home a place where we can more readily seize our destiny. ∎

THE TOP7 OF 2012
Austin, Texas, USA
A tale of two economies

■ ROBERT BELL, CO-FOUNDER, ICF

Austin is two cities overlaid on the same 300 square miles (777 km²) of central Texas, about 160 miles (257 km) west of the oil city of Houston.

One of these cities is a hotbed of innovation in information technology, telecommunications, transportation and energy, driven by the talents of graduates from the University of Texas, as well as the home of such American cultural icons as the South by Southwest (SXSW) music festival. It is also the state capital, with all of the economic and political power that implies. And it is the home of SEMATECH, a Federally-sponsored consortium of semiconductor manufacturers that, since 1988, has created advances in software development, manufacturing and clean technologies. SEMATECH is one reason why, back in the 1990s, direct flights between Austin and San Jose in Silicon Valley were dubbed the Nerd Birds.

In the other city, less than 5% of the population attends a college or university. Government, education, healthcare, tourism and retail are the primary employers. This is the population of people born and raised in Austin, 95% of whom fail to participate in the broadband economy despite the city's enviable 6.3% unemployment rate in the midst of recession.

In this contemporary tale of two cities, Austin is simultaneously striving to strengthen its position as a platform for tech innovation while also labouring to topple the barriers that block the majority of its citizens from opportunity.

The Recession-Proof Economy?

Austin already had a semiconductor manufacturing cluster in the 1980s when the SEMATECH consortium was founded to address fears that the US was losing its competitive edge in this crucial technology. But it is fair to say that SEMATECH accelerated the sector's growth by attracting research, development and manufacturing facilities to the city. Employment grew at an annual pace of nearly 5% in the 1990s and drove unemployment to as low as 2% by 1999. A decade of such growth led many to believe that Austin had become recession-proof.

The dot-com bust of 2000, which caused the loss of $5 billion in the market capitalization of US companies, put a stop to such talk. By 2004, the unemployment rate had surged to 6.7% amid a severe economic downturn. In response, the City of Austin partnered with the Greater Austin Chamber of Commerce to develop the first comprehensive economic development strategy for the five-county metropolitan area. The plan, called Opportunity Austin, aimed to put the region on the road to economic recovery after the loss of thousands of high-wage jobs.

Introduced in 2004, Opportunity Austin sought to create 72,000 new jobs and add $2.9 billion to the regional payroll by 2009. It focused on collaboration among Austin's outstanding university sector, business and government to stimulate business retention and growth.

One of its more successful efforts was the Emerging Technologies Program. Serving as a network and information clearinghouse, the ET program built partnerships among the Chamber, local incubators and skills development organizations to connect entrepreneurs to talent, advice, resources and funding.

It was also a relentless marketer of Austin as a home for the coolest of emerging technologies, which has engaged thousands of followers through active use of the tools of social media.

The ET program succeeded so well because it had many powerful assets to link with its network. Among them is the University of Texas at Austin and its internationally recognized computer science and technology programs. UT Austin graduates 13,000 students per year and is home to the IC^2 Institute, an interdisciplinary research unit founded in 1977. The Institute studies the theory and practice of entrepreneurial wealth creation – not a bad asset to have in a city that has bet its future on technology entrepreneurship. The Institute operates the Austin Technology Incubator, offers a Master of Science in Technology Commercialization and runs the Global Commercialization Group, which trains business people in venture incubation, global business acceleration and technology licensing. Since its founding in 1989, the Incubator alone has worked with over 200 companies and helped them raise over $750 million in investor capital. In the past three years, its alumni companies have realized over $300 million in exit value.

Opportunity Austin exceeded its creator's wildest expectations. Instead of creating 72,000 new jobs, it clocked

124,000 new jobs by 2009, and added $5.7 billion to regional payrolls, nearly double the $2.9 billion goal.

Austin In Brief

Population
812,025

Labor Force
436,336

Size
307.8 sq. mi.

Top Industries
Government, professional & business services, education & health services, leisure & hospitality, retail.

Broadband Penetration
83% household, 99% business, 100% govt.

Degrees Awarded
Community college 1,369; undergrad 10,926; graduate 5,038

3-Year Job Creation
28,860 (net 21,674); 4,799 depending on ICT

Key Leaders

Kevin Johns, Economic Development Director, City of Austin

Tim Crowley, President, Frost Bank

Isaac Barchas, Director, Austin Technology Incubator

Austin is now home to 3,300 technology companies with 100,000 employees, including Dell, Samsung Austin Semiconductor, Apple, IBM, Freescale Semiconductor, Advanced Micro Devices, Intel and Facebook. In addition to

IT, its tech companies and research facilities excel in life sciences, clean energy, wireless, and media and graphics.

The success of the first five-year plan led to Opportunity Austin 2.0, which seeks to create 117,000 more new jobs and add $10.8 billion to the region's payrolls by 2015. The city is well on the way: in the past three recessionary years, Austin has already added nearly 27,000 new jobs.

Building the Other Economy

The supposedly recession-proof economy of the 1990s was based on a vital import: talented students entering UT Austin, St. Edwards University, Concordia University or one of the region's other institutions of higher learning. With the local economy offering so much opportunity, many chose to stay and prosper. But the native born lived in a completely different economy, largely cut off from opportunity by poor educational attainment, low expectations and a culture that did not encourage upward mobility.

Austin has attacked this problem with energy and ambition. Focusing on secondary school, the Chamber of Commerce tapped business, public education and government leaders to form a Matriculation Task Force. The Task Force created and funded a program called "20,010 by 2010," which focused on ways to increase the metropolitan area's university enrollment by 20,010 more students through 2010. Though the initiative, many schools hired College Enrollment Managers, who advise students on how to get into college, including the filing of the Federal application for student aid known as FAFSA. By October of 2011, 21,000 more Austin Metro students were enrolled in post-secondary education, including community college and technical schools. While saluting the attainment of another goal, the Chamber also estimates that 75% of jobs becoming available in central Texas through 2018 will require higher education. To meet that need, the Chamber set a new goal: to increase higher education enrollment to 100,000 or 6% of the homegrown population, by 2015.

Another partnership between the Chamber and the Austin Independent School District (AISD) aimed at ensuring that Austin students graduate "college and career ready." In 2009, AISD approved a strategic plan that called for the district to graduate 90 percent of the Class of 2014 and ensure that 77% of them enrolled in higher education. For the Class of 2009, the overall graduation rate was 76%, and the proportion of graduates who were college and career ready was 50%, unchanged from the prior year.

> Like all overachievers, Austin believes there is another mountain to climb and is in a big hurry to conquer it.

Clearly there is more work to do, but in an encouraging sign, the graduation rate of low-income students jumped 14% to 75% overall.

From Work to a Career

Austin's efforts do not stop with secondary school. The Skillpoint Alliance of government, business and institutions provides training that aims to equip secondary-school graduates for careers as electricians, computer technicians and office administrators. It operates Community Technology Training Centers to equip young people for a workforce in which 70% of jobs require digital technology skills. The program graduates 90% of its students, and 80% of graduates are successful in finding work.

The city invests over $1 million per year in Capital IDEA, a nonprofit partnership of employers and community-based organizations that prepare low-earning adults for higher-value careers. Its board is made up of senior executives of the metro area's technology companies. It has placed nearly 900 program graduates in careers including electronic technicians, power utility technicians, network administrators, solar power technicians and health care technicians. Studies of the program show large gains in employment, and a 17% annual return for taxpayers. A survey by a Southwestern University student documented further impacts on the children of Capital IDEA graduates, including a 90% secondary school graduation rate and 65% university enrollment rate.

Austin has also invested more than $1 million over 10 years in the Grant for Technology Opportunities Program (GTOP). It provides matching grants to Austin organizations for projects that create digital opportunities and foster digital inclusion. GTOP has served nearly 22,000 individuals with computer training, media production, Internet access and micro-enterprise management programs. Its grantees have raised more than $2.3 million in matching funds including 24,000 volunteer hours.

Austin Free-Net is a nonprofit created by the city in 1994 to provide technology training and broadband access. It operates 15 community sites where citizens receive training and free broadband access, and averages 6,700 users per month. Like most US cities, Austin also operates public-access cable TV channels. But ChannelAustin, as the channels are branded, also offers a comprehensive video production training program and studio and production facilities with state-of-the-art equipment. Fees are kept low and scholarships and internships are available. At any given them, there are 475 producers working at ChannelAustin, which offers special programs for at-risk youth and collaborative programs with schools and local nonprofits.

Blueberry in the Tomato Soup

Austin is a politically liberal city in a conservative state, or a "blueberry in a bowl of tomato soup" in contemporary American political jargon. Its political and social culture admits a degree of government activism and government-business-institutional collaboration that can be difficult to achieve in the USA.

Its history with broadband is indicative. In 1994, Austin proposed a city-wide broadband network similar in concept to Google's Fiber to Communities proposal of 2010. It helped spark a national discussion of the proper role for cities in such projects, but created a victory for the private sector when the state ruled that only business could build and operate such a network. By 2002, Austin was at it again with a plan to have a business partner build a fiber network within the city's stormwater drainage system. The business deal fell through, during a period when municipal network projects were running into headwinds across America. Another deal negotiated at the same time, however, led a private partner to install fiber-optic ductwork in the downtown core to serve the long-term needs of telecom providers.

But in the meantime, the broadband market evolved, and a metropolis like Austin was at the top of the deployment list for carriers. As owner of its own electric utility and 90% of utility poles, Austin encouraged deployment by offering a master pole attachment agreement. Today, it is one of the top three most wired communities in the country, with an 83% broadband penetration rate for homes and 99% for businesses and government.

Austin is the envy of most communities, with its powerful and growing tech sector, its rich educational infrastructure, and creative and cultural assets including the South by Southwest Music Festival and Film & Interactive Conference, which together inject over $100 million into the economy per year. But Austin measures its success by a different yardstick. Compared with the great granddaddy of technology clusters, Silicon Valley, Austin sees itself struggling with commercialization and funding. It has one of the nation's highest levels of new patents, but has no Sand Hill Road in Menlo Park, where Silicon Valley's venture capital firms cluster and provide the fuel for innovation. Like all overachievers, Austin believes there is another mountain to climb and is in a big hurry to conquer it. ∎

PLATFORMS FOR INNOVATION
What Innovation Means – And What It Doesn't

■ ROBERT BELL, CO-FOUNDER, ICF

In his 2007 book, *Innovation Nation*, Harvard professor John Kao wrote that:

> *Robert Solow won the Nobel Prize in economics for, among other things, demonstrating that as much as 80 percent of GDP growth comes through the introduction of new technology. And the Boston Consulting Group, in a study conducted for BusinessWeek, concluded that innovative companies achieved median profit margin growth of 3.4 percent as compared with 0.4 percent for the median S&P Global 1200.*[1]

Those figures should startle you. Eighty percent of economic growth comes from new technology? That's terrible news for the vast majority of communities which are not cranking out iPad apps or revolutionary new batteries for electric cars. They are doomed to sharing scraps from the table – the 20% of growth that is not generated by the high technology.

But of course, that's not the reality. Innovation is all too easily confused today with high tech, because the industries spawned by our ability to turn silicon into semiconductors have generated one of history's greatest waves of innovation.

According to Gregory Gromov's 2010 book, *From the Gold Mines of El Dorado to the 'Golden' Startups of Silicon Valley*, the high-tech phenomenon centered on San Jose, California got its start because a company's founder could not get along with his employees:

> *The spark that set off the explosive boom of "Silicon startups" in Stanford Industrial Park was a personal dispute in 1957 between employees of Shockley Semiconductor and the company's namesake and founder, Nobel laureate and co-inventor of the transistor William Shockley... (His employees) formed Fairchild Semiconductor immediately following their departure... After several years, Fairchild gained its footing, becoming a formidable presence in this sector. Its founders began to leave to start companies based on their own, latest ideas and were followed on this path by their own former leading employees... The process gained momentum and what had once begun in a Stanford research park became a veritable startup avalanche... Thus, over the course of just 20 years, a mere eight of Shockley's former employees brought forth 65 new enterprises, which then went on to do the same...* [2]

Information technology has shown two remarkable abilities since the founding days of Silicon Valley: to reduce its own cost year after year, and to reduce the cost of every process that incorporates it. When the cost of something useful decreases, we tend to use more of it. The mobile phone is the most successful technology device in history precisely because of this dynamic. In 2009, there were more than four billion mobile phone subscriptions worldwide, outpacing fixed lines by nearly four times.[3] In February 2011, Cisco reported that global mobile phone traffic had tripled over the previous 12 months – for the third year in a row.[4] If we have come to think of innovation and information technology as synonyms, it is because the ever-falling cost and ever-growing power of IT has made it the world's coolest sandbox, in which technologists can build castles to their heart's content.

Innovation Is Not About Technology

But innovation and technology are not the same things at all.

One of the greatest innovations in business history was an idea: the limited liability corporation or joint-stock company, which arose in Europe in the 13th Century. The joint-stock company gave investors two big benefits: protection from individual liability for losses and a ready means to turn their ownership interest into cash by selling it to someone else. It triggered a centuries-long rise in trade and went on to become the financial and legal foundation of the Industrial Revolution.

Eleven centuries earlier, Chinese innovators came up with a very different idea: pulverizing plant fibers, mixing them with water, and then straining the result through a flat mesh or screen. When dried and pressed, the result was paper. Over the next thousand years, it revolutionized record-keeping and communications around the world.

> Innovation is about coming up with a better process, creating a new product, improving an existing one, opening a new market, finding a new source of supply or a creating a better way to organize ourselves.

In 1901, the Coca-Cola Company was selling its sugary syrup base to restaurants and drug stores, where it was mixed with carbonated water at the point of sale. Then a group of young businessmen in the city of Chattanooga, Tennessee, USA, persuaded Coke to sell them the right to pre-mix and bottle Coke. So skeptical was the company of their success that it sold the rights for $1. The businessmen turned that modest investment into a nationwide empire of bottling plants that sparked the global distribution of today. [5]

To innovate means literally to renew or change something. Innovation is about coming up with a better process, creating a new product, improving an existing one, opening a new market, finding a new source of supply or a creating a better way to organize ourselves. Innovation may be technology-driven but it is just as likely to focus on a new and better way for people to work together.

The important thing about innovation is that it creates economic value. In fact, according to management consultant Peter Drucker, the only business activities that create value are *innovation* (making something new) and *marketing* (finding a way to sell it). Everything else we do is a cost that must be paid from the proceeds of innovation and marketing.[6] That explains the finding of Boston Consulting, cited by Professor Kao above, that innovative companies grow their profits at more than eight times the rate of companies that do not. The wages paid and the profits made by innovative employers generate the economic energy that powers everything else in the communities we live in.

Innovation is Not Invention

If innovation is not the same as technology, it should also not be confused with invention – though it usually is. A wit once observed that invention involves turning cash into ideas, whereas innovation is about turning ideas into cash. And that's a good thing. Very few communities are hotbeds of invention, and the overwhelming majority of inventions produce no economic benefit. The US Patent & Trademark Office estimates that only one of out every 500 patents has the remotest trace of commercial potential. [7] How many find their way to successful product launches? One in 3,000? One in 5,000? No one knows for sure but those are the guesses made by experts.

Where a successful technology, product or service is invented turns out to have almost no bearing on who benefits economically from it. A 2009 report from McKinsey & Company, *Where Innovation Creates Value*, pours cold water on the notion that, because an increasing number of inventions are coming from outside the United States, America is doomed to economic decline. The same logic applies to any advanced economy where both leaders and citizens obsess about the need to raise the rate of new inventions.

> Invention involves turning cash into ideas, whereas innovation is about turning ideas into cash.

The transistor was patented by two German scientists. But it was not until William Shockley – he who could not get along with his employees – created an improved version and licensed it to American companies that the transistor revolutionized electronics. The World Wide Web's protocols were invented by an Englishman working in a Swiss lab, but the economic benefit has spread throughout the world.

The study's author, Amar Bhide, points out that that the US state of Maryland "has a higher per capita income than

Mississippi not because Maryland is or was an extremely significant developer of breakthrough technologies but because of its greater ability to benefit from them. Conversely, the city of Rochester in New York state – home to Kodak and Xerox – is reputed to have one of the highest per capita levels of patents of all US cities. It is far from the most economically vibrant among them, however." [8]

Innovation for All

It is good news for communities that innovation is not necessarily about technology. It is also good news that innovation is not the same as invention. Try as they might, most communities will not transform themselves into hotbeds of technology invention. But there is every opportunity for communities to raise the innovation rate of their businesses, institutions and government. Information and communications technology (ICT) are almost certain to play a role, because of their power to help us do everything cheaper, faster and better. Economist Robert Solow showed that the introduction of new technology produces as much as 80% of GDP growth. But notice the choice of words: "introduction," not "invention." Long before the Silicon Gold Rush attracted technologists and investors to Silicon Valley, the California Gold Rush drew prospectors from around the world to that US state in search of instant wealth. Most never found it. Who prospered the most overall? The tradesman and manufacturers who supplied them with tools, clothing, food and drink. The "introduction" of gold into the California economy did indeed provide an outrageous boost to gross domestic product, but not in the way that anyone expected. ∎

THE TOP7 OF 2012
Oulu, Finland
Riding the waves of change

■ ROBERT BELL, CO-FOUNDER, ICF

The cycles of life are strong in Oulu, a coastal city at the northern end of the Baltic Sea. Located only 200 km south of the Arctic Circle, the city experiences long, snowy winters, when there are only six hours of daylight in December, punctuated by short, warm summers when nature seems to roar back to life.

Oulu's economy has also seen its share of cycles. Tar and wooden sailing ships were its primary products in the 1800s but the rise of steel vessels in the 1890s gradually eliminated its markets. Leather goods took their place until the 1930s, when salmon fishing also declined as electric power stations were built on the Oulu River. Heavy equipment manufacturing for the forestry sector boomed after the Second World War but fell victim to rising globalization in the 1970s.

By then the cycles were coming faster and faster. After the recession of the Seventies, the telecommunications sector led by the handset maker Nokia grew at a robust pace. By 1990, the Nokia Research Center and its small to midsize vendors (SMEs) were the city's most important employer. The dot-com recession of the 1990s, plus the collapse of the

Soviet Union as an export market, sparked another downturn that led to substantial job losses.

The 21st Century has been no gentler. Massive competitive pressure from Chinese mobile technology firms, and the rise of the smartphone market led by Apple, caught Nokia flat-footed. When the financial crisis of 2007 struck, the company was forced into restructuring and layoffs that struck Oulu hard. That explains why the city has seen a net increase of only 300 jobs in the past three years despite having created nearly 7,000 new positions.

Yet through the accelerating waves of change, Oulu has built a reputation as one of the most innovative tech centers in Europe, a place of many "firsts" in the relentless march of improvement in information and communications technology (ICT). It has done so, not by unleashing the Darwinian forces of raw capitalism, but by turning Oulu into a living, breathing laboratory in which business, government and citizens each play a vital part.

The PanOULU Network

The innovation engine in Oulu is not unlike the DNA in your body. You function as a living, breathing whole in part because each cell in your body contains all of the genetic instructions for making a new you. That is how projects tend to go in Oulu, and there is no better example than PanOULU.

On the face of it, it is simple enough: a wireless broadband network that covers the main parts of the city, university campus areas and such high traffic areas as Oulu's airport. It is an open network offering free service to all – no surprise in a nation where access to the Internet has been declared a human right. With about 25,000 users per month at the end of 2011, PanOULU is growing usage by about 25% per year.

Oulu In Brief

Population
142,000

Labor Force
89,000

Size
450 km^2

Top Industries
Health and social services; ICT, professional and busi-ness services; education and public administration; manufacturing, mining and utilities.

Broadband Penetration
80% household, 90% business, 100% govt & nonprofit.

Degrees Awarded
Community college 2,372; undergrad 3,011; graduate 1,656.

3-Year Job Creation
6,750 (300 net), 1,800 depending on ICT.

Key Leaders
Juha Ala-Mursula, Executive Director, BusinessOulu

Juha Juntunen, Senior Vice President, Technopolis Group

Heikki Huomo, Director, Center for Internet Excellence

But look inside PanOULU, and you see the unique pattern of innovation in Oulu. The network was born in 2003 when 17 organizations pooled their WiFi networks into a single managed platform. The City of Oulu was the largest player, with 600 access points covering its downtown and public facilities. Eight other nearby townships also joined in. But local governments were not the only players.

Oulu is home to a number of institutions that have, over past decades, built global footprints. The University of Oulu is the second largest in Finland, with 16,000 students. It focuses on information technology, biotech and environmental sciences, and its Innovation Services unit has helped spawn 35 successful startups since 2001 as well as an annual stream of patent applications, tech transfer agreements and licensing agreements.

The University joined PanOULU, as did the Oulu University of Applied Sciences, a well-regarded 2-year institution. Another member was the VTT Technical Research Center of Finland. VTT is the biggest contract research organization in northern Europe, with annual turnover of about €290 million and over 3,000 employees. It exists to commercialize new inventions, from helping refine business ideas to connecting entrepreneurs with knowledge and funding.

There is another organization that is not part of PanOULU but is nonetheless a vital part of the community's innovation system. Technopolis Plc is a publicly-traded operator of technology centers in Finland and Russia. Founded in 1982 by city government, Technopolis provides facilities and services to spur the growth of knowledge-intensive companies. One of its programs, conducted jointly with Nokia and Tekes (a national funding program for technology), is called the Innovation Mill. It offers thousands of Nokia's unused ideas and intellectual property rights to companies that can turn them into products and services benefiting Oulu.

The company is also part of the Oulu Innovation Alliance (OIA), which counts most of PanOULU's participants among its members. OIA aims to maintain Oulu's intensive collaboration among academia, industry and the public sector. It has established five innovation centers – from the Center for Internet Excellence to the Center of Expertise in the Water Industry – to build Oulu's economic strength.

These organizations, with their different but complementary missions, move in a remarkable dance of collaboration. In 2004, Oulu celebrated its 400th anniversary with a new program called Competence Oulu 400. It aimed to expand PanOULU's reach both in geographic and human terms. Four hundred new access points were added as well as 100 public Internet kiosks. To improve citizen's skills, the program training packages and programs, which have educated more than 9,000 mostly elderly residents. The partners joined forces in 2007 to lobby the Finnish association that manages the country's Internet exchanges. In 2008, the association opened its third Internet Exchange Point in Oulu, which substantially improved the quality of IP backbone connectivity and created the opportunity for Oulu to host data centers.

Inside an Innovation Strategy

Like its neighboring states in northern Europe, Finland is a believer in big government, with high taxation that funds comprehensive social services. The City of Oulu is the largest employer and service provider in its region, and its decisions have profound impact on the economy of the metropolitan area.

The city's 2007-13 Innovation Strategy stresses the importance of human enthusiasm as a source of innovation.

The strategy rests on several key assumptions: that the region has ambitious businesses, that opportunities will arise from connecting them with the potential of the global market, and that services will gain an increasing role in economic growth. But there is another assumption that distinguishes Oulu from many other places. It is that citizens of all ages should be involved in business and institutional innovation.

From 2006 to 2008, the SmartTouch project conducted research in eight European countries on near-field communications, which allows devices like mobile phones to interact when placed next to each other and may power a new generation of retail e-commerce. Oulu was the only government body in SmartTouch that found ways to connect ICT companies directly to its citizens. Participating in ten pilot projects, Oulu residents tried out the technology in everything from a school environmental project to cultural and senior citizen services.

SmartTouch met with such enthusiasm that the community created, in 2010, the Oulu Urban Living Labs (OULLabs), a network that enables testing of products and services in real environments with authentic users. Citizens engage in OULLabs by registering for the online PATIO user community, where they can participate in testing and also contribute to the design of new applications and services. They can volunteer to join programs like the Technology Healthcare Center, in which PATIO users provide a testbed for companies to conduct usability testing, user studies, interviews and pilot programs in healthcare technologies.

> In Oulu, innovation has a powerful role in dealing with the downsides of globalization.

And it is not all about business. The OmaOulu Citizens Portal provides one-stop access to a broad range of citizen services, from applications and procedures to personalized health services. In 2007, Oulu launched an online platform called eYouthwork, which provides real-time chats in which young people converse with each other and youth workers. By 2011, eYouthwork was serving some 25,000 young people per year. One successful services is eJepari ("e-cop" in English), in which young people can converse anonymously with a police officer and youth worker on topics from drugs and education to violence and traffic laws. A typical eJepari chat has 350 participants.

Connecting Point

BusinessOulu, the economic development agency of the city, is the center point around which much of this activity revolves. BusinessOulu works to ease access to the networks of business and institutions in the region, access to talent, access to R&D resources, and access to funding from European Union, national and local sources. It taps Finnish government programs aimed at developing specific clusters, from health and wellness to ubiquitous computing. It offers start-up services, training and acceleration services, support for international marketing and sales, and guidance to international companies seeking investment opportunities in Oulu.

Its work and those of Oulu's many innovation groups have helped to create Oulu's life sciences cluster, where 180 companies turn over €300m on such technologies as the world's first consumer heart rate monitor, miniature electrodes for neuroscience and cardiac muscle research, and consumer genetic tests. In clean technology, Oulu boasts 60 companies with €400m in turnover, which have developed ways to print electronic components for solar cells and paper-like displays, as well as ways to pre-treat wood chips to reduce the energy consumption of industrial processes.

Elektrobit, founded in Oulu in 1985, now employs 1,600 people in seven countries, developing wireless technologies and advanced embedded electronics for the automotive industry. Codenomicon is a prime example of a successful research spin-off. Founded in 2001, it provides tools for the automated testing of network protocols for companies including Alcatel-Lucent, Microsoft, Sony-Ericsson and Nokia Siemens Networks.

And innovation has an equally powerful role in dealing with the downside of globalization. The leaders of Oulu now speak of the "Nokia risk" – the realization that a single dominant company poses risks as well as presenting opportunities to the economy. When Nokia announced layoffs of 1,400 staff in 2011, many of them in Oulu, the company also created the Bridge program. It provides support to employees seeking a job outside the company, returning to school or starting a business. In Oulu, all of the innovation partners have collaborated intensively with Nokia and affected staff to ensure that local talent stays in the community and finds a prosperous future.

In 2013, Oulu will merge with surrounding townships to create a single municipality with more than 183,000 inhabitants. The move will present major new challenges. But this is a community that has seen repeated challenges, generation after generation. For Oulu, it is yet another opportunity to ride the waves of change into a successful future. ■

PLATFORMS FOR INNOVATION
How Intelligent Communities Create Innovation Ecosystems
■ ROBERT BELL, CO-FOUNDER, ICF

Intelligent Communities word hard to create a climate for innovation, and then letting their businesses, institutions and citizens make it happen.

What factors create that climate? There are four essential inputs: access to knowledge, talent, markets and money.

Access to Knowledge
We tend to think of innovation as beginning with a blank sheet of paper. The whiteboard covered with notes and equations has become the popular symbol of the creative process, which starts when smart people go into a room and brainstorm the Next Big Thing.

But real innovation begins with detailed knowledge of what has been done before. Nobody is going to light up the world by going to the whiteboard, storming their brains out and announcing their world-changing idea: a telephone without wires that you can stick in your pocket. A great idea, but that particular ship has already sailed.

It should be no surprise, therefore, that so much innovation has come from university-business collaboration. Colleges and universities are repositories for knowledge, and academic research always begins with a search for what has been done before in a particular field of study. So Intelligent

Communities engage with their institutions of higher learning and foster their ties to business. They stage conferences and networking events to bring the two sides together. They promote intellectual property policies that encourage academics to create new companies. They support business incubation programs and the development of institutes to generate knowledge in areas with economic potential.

And what of the majority of communities that are not home to a college or university? That is where ICT can have a profound impact. Web access, distance learning and online collaboration tools can vastly expand access to knowledge, whether general knowledge of innovation taking place elsewhere or relationships with specific innovation leaders in business and academia. Technical or community colleges can also play a role as a bridge between local entrepreneurs and the broader academic community, using the same digital tools. It is hardly a substitute for hanging out at the campus of one of the world's leading universities, but it represents a huge advance in opportunity for communities around the world.

> Much innovation comes from university-business collaboration.

Access to Talent

When it comes to innovation, the scarcest natural resource is talent: skilled, knowledgeable people, who can think creatively, execute in a disciplined way and collaborate effectively with others. The more we innovate, the more specialized our talent requirements become – so much so that a single community, even a major city, is increasingly unlikely to meet them all.

In *Innovation Nation*, Harvard's John Kao relates the story of what he calls "weightless companies [whose] gossamer scale and agility go hand in glove with the ability to exploit the advantages of globalization. Jim Hornthal, a San Francisco venture capitalist, for example, is nurturing a new venture in his one-man incubator at the San Francisco Presidio. His designer is in Japan, his front-end coding team is in Bangalore, his back-end programmers are in Russia, and he has a team of contractors sprinkled around the world. Most of these professionals remain faceless to Jim; he has never met them in person. And Jim intends to make use of Amazon's EC2 platform – short for Elastic Compute Cloud – which provides infrastructure, support and distribution capability, leveraging off Amazon's corporate assets. When a venture capitalist asked him how much the start-up was costing him, Jim said 'Three.' Oh, $3 million, came the reply. No, said Jim, $300,000."

Creating a new Web company obviously plays to the strengths of such online collaboration, while most businesses and institutions require much more face-to-face engagement of talented people. Intelligent Communities support this need with talent attraction programs focused on specific industries, and on talent development programs that motivate young people leaving university to locate in the community rather than taking their talents elsewhere. They also work to create a local culture that welcomes, affirms and entertains the creative knowledge workers who drive innovation.

Access to Markets

The folks with that whiteboard can think up all the fantastic innovations they want, but until they find paying customers, the innovations have no economic value. Most cities began life as markets where people went to trade goods, and market access remains the lifeblood of innovative communities. But in the 21st Century, the market that innovators need to access is much larger: the size of states or provinces, nations or the entire globe.

So Intelligent Communities develop and manage projects that connect local companies with prospective customers in government, the nonprofit sector and regional businesses. They provide education and support to local companies on regulatory, legal and international business issues. They even take on the role of ambassadors who work to build trade connections on behalf of their businesses with communities throughout their region, country or in targeted other countries.

Access to Money

Most companies are founded for the purpose of "income replacement" – to provide a job for the entrepreneur who starts them. But a percentage of small businesses are what MIT researcher David Birch termed "gazelles" – nimble, aggressive start-ups with big ambitions hungry for the resources needed to achieve them. Successful "gazelles" create the employment growth on which the rest of the local economy feeds.

> Successful "gazelles" create the employment growth that on which the rest of the local economy feeds.

And they need investment capital to realize their dreams, whether it is public-sector grants or loans, "friends & family" and angel investing by individuals, or early stage and venture financing by professionally-managed funds.

For most communities, this is one of the toughest challenges of innovation. Capital does not grow on trees. Except for major cities and established innovation regions, professional investors are scarce. Intelligent Communities seek to fill the gap by educating their potential "gazelles" on available funding programs provided by national and regional governments. They help angel investors to organize investor networks that expose them to more opportunities. They create public-private investment funds of their own that serve two vital purposes: providing seed financing for promising startups while also developing relationships with professional investors and guiding their best portfolio companies to later stages of funding.

Innovation Leadership

Intelligent Communities also make more subtle but powerful contributions to the creation of an innovation ecosystem.

They lead by example. The governments of Intelligent Communities are innovators in the use of ICT to improve service to citizens and employers while simultaneously reducing the costs of government. They invest in an amazing range of online services and processes delivered through the Web as well as smartphones. Putting effective government systems online drives the adoption of a broadband culture of use in the community and signals to innovative individuals and companies that this community is ahead of the curve.

They also celebrate innovation in ways large and small. Local governments and institutions have great power to shape culture through what they choose to honor publicly. So Intelligent Communities hold Entrepreneur Weeks and Technology Festivals, Fiber Fetes and Digital Challenges. They apply for awards and digital rankings, and then celebrate when they are winners. They make local heroes of innovators in businesses and institutions to make clear just how vital to the community's future their efforts are. ∎

THE TOP7 OF 2012
Quebec City, Quebec, Canada
Turning a provincial capital into a global magnet for talent

■ ROBERT BELL, CO-FOUNDER, ICF

In English-speaking countries, a person born to wealth is said to be born with a silver spoon in the mouth.

The capital cities of states, provinces and nations tend to be born with that silver spoon, because they are places where decisions on a government's countless programs are made, with large sums of money at stake.

But sometimes, they wind up choking on it. The problem arises when government dominates the economy, squeezing out any activity that is not about legislating, lobbing or lawyering. Government is not a net creator of prosperity, after all – it recycles and redirects money that is already in the economy. When it becomes too dominant a part of the economic mix, the result can be stagnation.

That was the problem faced by Quebec City, capital of the Canadian province of Quebec, in 2000. Founded in the early 17th century on the banks of the St. Lawrence River, Quebec City retains an Old World charm, reflected in its designation as a UNESCO World Heritage Site. It is also one of Canada's greenest cities, where more than half of the land is forested.

Twelve year ago, economically speaking, Quebec City had government and all the private-sector activity that government attracts. It had heavy manufacturing, but that was experiencing the same slow erosion of employment seen throughout the industrial world as companies pursued higher productivity and lower costs. Despite considerable effort to attract high-tech firms, there was simply no sector of the economy that offered real growth prospects. In 1998, the entire Quebec City region was home to only 75 high-tech companies, which accounted for just 3% of the province's high-tech jobs.

And then, in 2001, the tech bubble burst. It wasn't the most auspicious time to launch a tech-based economic development strategy. But that is precisely what Quebec City did.

Strategy for Growth

The new strategy targeted the success factors for 21st Century economic growth that ICF calls its Intelligent Community Indicators. It called for diversifying the economy into high-value, high-skill businesses, increasing the contribution of education and training to the economy, and improving quality of life for residents. The plan received a helpful boost from a provincial effort, launched in 2002, to promote innovation in ICT, insurance and financial services, life sciences, health foods and green and intelligent buildings. This was backed by an US$18 million Innovation Fund for seeding new companies and growing established ones, which leveraged a further $9 million from private sources.

As it turned out, Quebec City had all the necessary resources for the job. All that had been missing were a strong vision and sustained attention. Now political leaders, administrative officials, university presidents and business executives were ready to act – and to act together.

For example, the city had owned a technology business park since 1988. But it was not until 1999, when a new public-private leadership team converted it into an independent nonprofit, that it started living up to its potential. Today, the Quebec Metro High Tech Park contains nearly 100 companies and research organizations, and has a workforce of 5,000.

This growth was nourished by more than 20 universities and community colleges operating in the city. They provided fertile ground for a strategy aiming at building knowledge-intensive businesses. About 90% of the working age population has at least a secondary school diploma. Community college enrollment exceeds 30,000 and 45,000 university students make the city #2 in North America for its college population.

These resources, as well as the city's status as a provincial capital, made it an attractive place for the national government to locate research centers. DRDC Valcartier, located in Quebec City, is Canada's largest defense research facility. Private companies are partners in one-half of its R&D programs, and the resulting intellectual property has found its way to market in numerous products and services.

The National Optics Institute is one of Canada's biggest applied research facilities. Since the 1980s, it has carried out 50 technology transfers to industry and generated more than 25 spin-off companies. One example, Creaform, was founded in 2002 and has since become a world leader in 3D scanning and digitization.

This growth was nourished by more than 20 universities and community colleges operating in the city. They provided fertile ground for a strategy aiming at building knowledge-intensive businesses. About 90% of the working age population has at least a secondary school diploma. Community

---

Quebec City In Brief

Population
548,875

Labor Force
271,690

Size
454 km²

Top Industries
Government, automotive, household services, manufacturing, construction.

Broadband Penetration
95% households, 100% business, 100% government, 100% education.

Degrees Awarded
Community college 7,155; undergrad 7,766; graduate 3,427.

3-Year Job Creation
22,833, 3,015 depending on ICT.

Key Leaders

Carl Viel, CEO, Quebec International

Christian Goulet, AVP, Quebec Public Sector, Bell Canada

David Pelletier, Coordinator, ZAP Quebec

---

college enrollment exceeds 30,000 and 45,000 university students make the city #2 in North America for its college population.

These resources, as well as the city's status as a provincial capital, made it an attractive place for the national government to locate research centers. DRDC Valcartier, located in Quebec City, is Canada's largest defense research facility. Private companies are partners in one-half of its R&D programs, and the resulting intellectual property has found its way to market in numerous products and services.

The National Optics Institute is one of Canada's biggest applied research facilities. Since the 1980s, it has carried out 50 technology transfers to industry and generated more than 25 spin-off companies. One example, Creaform, was founded in 2002 and has since become a world leader in 3D scanning and digitization.

The Infectiology Research Center at Laval University has about 250 scientists on staff, who have filed for 40 patents and helped create several companies. Newly-funded firms include Atrium Innovations, which creates and commercializes science-based natural health products, and Medicago, which develops affordable vaccines.

Accelerating Change

Change is like a big rock rolling down a hill. It is difficult to get started and slow-moving at first. But gravity exerts a constant acceleration and the rock's momentum at the bottom of the hill can be tremendous.

In the 20 years to 2009, employment in professional, scientific and technical service sectors more than doubled from 12,700 to 27,800. By 2005, medium-to-high knowledge jobs made up 38% of all jobs in the local economy. By 2007, the unemployment rate was down to 4.5%, half of what it had been in 2000.

In 2008, city government introduced 1888 Me Voilà, a one-stop online service center providing information and referrals to support companies recruiting foreign workers and foreign workers looking for a position. One hundred thirty thousand visitors from 160 countries have used the site, and the wages paid to new hires have contributed US$58 million to the economy.

In the same year, the region adopted a program called Devtech to improve the success rate of tech companies. It offers consulting and professional development for entrepreneurs, financial assistance, entepreneurial competitions and growth accelerator programs. Since 2008, it has served 225 companies and generated US$15m in new investment.

Lavall University committed, in 2008, to a goal of creating 100 new research chairs and securing $100 million in new investment over five years. Two years later, it had notched up 26 research chairs and $120m in investment from external partners.

The National School of Interactive Entertainment (ENDI) opened in 2008 to offer students a place to hone their video game development skills in an environment combining production techniques and a corporate immersion program. ENDI forges closer ties and better alignment between the educational sectors and the needs of Quebec City's growing gaming sector. Its students enjoy a job placement rate of 83%, with 60% of graduates hired in the region. Some of them go to work for Frima, Canada's largest video game and digital entertainment studio. Founded in 2003, the company has 350 employees and, from 2005 to 2009, posted annual growth of 3,000%. In addition to original products, the company develops Web games, virtual universes, concept art, animation and special effects for the video game, film and TV markets.

There is more than education, however, to nurturing creative industries. Online technology, arts and culture organizations have clustered over the past decade in a neighborhood called Saint Roch. When the recession struck in 2008, the city began to focus generous subsidy and incentive programs on the neighborhood to support arts centers, galleries and entertainment venues. A total of US$50m over five years is paying for outdoor productions by Cirque du Soleil and Robert LePage to anchor the neighborhood, a "technoculture" investment fund for digital arts companies and a 100% tax credit for new construction or renovation. The city estimates that this investment will help to create or maintain 30,000 jobs.

> Quebec City's next challenge: to transform itself from a city of beauty, charm and brains into an global magnet for talent.

Broadband Density

Communities like Quebec City seldom have trouble attracting communications carriers willing to install broadband. Since 2010, competitive operators have invested close to half a billion dollars in the region. Incumbent Bell Canada, which is headquartered in Quebec, will deploy fiber to 240,000 homes over utility poles by the end of 2012. Telus is investing $250 milion in extending and upscaling its wireline and wireless offerings. They may be responding to the success of a newer player, Videotron, which has deployed 4G wireless to 80% of the city, covering 310,000 homes and business locations. A service upgrade announced in August 2011 will provide speeds of up to 42 Mbps.

But even this kind of robust broadband asset fails to reach everyone. To address issues of affordability, the city government and private-sector partners set up a nonprofit organization called ZAP Quebec to build a free wireless network. Municipal and provincial government pay for equipment and connections, but ZAP Quebec is entirely volunteer-run and operated. Since its founding, ZAP Quebec has installed 431 Internet access points covering 62% of the population. More than 5,000 people per day use the network, and unique visitors have grown an average of 40% per year. Some of that growth has come from local merchants, who have shrewdly begun to capitalize on the availability of ubiquitious broadband and applications like Foursquare and Facebook to build customers. The 2011 Quebec City Summer Festival recorded more than 37,000 connections, compared with 3,500 the previous year.

Faster into the Future

In 2010 and 2011, the rolling stone of change picked up more speed. Quebec City partnered with six other universities and the Quebec Science Information Network to launch the Quebec Intermunicipal Network. It provides each city government with dedicated 250 Mbps of capacity on dual fiber links, and a shared 600 Mbps connection. Participating cities have seen their telecom costs slashed by 85%. It will also enable the cities to share muncipal IT services and applications like payroll, human resources and support for municipal courts.

The city also launched an interactive Web map providing high-quality cartographic and zoning data. After implementation, calls to city departments from notaries, surveyors, lawyers and real estate agents fell by 50%. The map also displays in real time the location of the city's snow plows. Through smarter deployment of plows, the city has been able to reduce the number of vehicles and operating expenses per vehicle while providing better results.

Once a community's innovation engine is moving this fast, it tends to take on a life of its own. In 2010, the metro area's many research centers formed a new organization, the Quebec City Regional Association for Innovation and Technology Development. Its first project was Quebec Seeks Solutions, a "jam" in which a diverse group of researchers met for a day to tackle a list of tough technical problems proposed by private companies. The challenges ranged from creating a "smart helmet" for urban bicycle riders to building a network of sensors able to analyze fast-changing and complex phenomena. The 160 attendees came up with enough interesting ideas that most submitting companies planned to pursue solutions based on them and three signed NDAs with participants.

The city's Web development community joined in with Web à Québec, an annual event that offers professional development to practitioners and publicizes the importance of Web applications to Québécois, as residents are known. Addressing both goals, the "Iron Web" competition locks two teams into a room for 48 hours to design, from scratch, a finished Web site, with live Webcam coverage throughout.

The city followed suit in 2011 by organizing a Hackathon that opened selected public computer data for use by Web designers and programmers. Prototypes created during the event included a tool for avoiding road construction around the city and another for locating a nearby parking space.

Quebec City in 2012 is a very different place from the city of 2000. Despite the recession that began in 2008, regional GDP has grown from $20 billion to $26 billion as the region has added over 13,000 new jobs. From 2005 to 2010, 74% of new jobs were medium-to-high skilled, and robust growth in the private sector actually shrank the public sector's share of jobs from 36% to 34%. There has also been a net increase in both international and internal migration, with more than 4,600 new arrivals in 2010 alone. The immigration retention rate of Quebec City is 85%.

High immigration is good news, for a shortage of qualified workers has become the city's new leading problem. Technology companies feel it most deeply and are hungry for senior managers, professionals, technicians, project managers and IT support. If Quebec City is to keep seizing its destiny, it will have to raise its game again: to transform itself from a city of beauty, charm and brains into an global magnet for talent. ■

REFLECTION ON THE
INTELLIGENT COMMUNITY OF THE YEAR
How They Seized Their Destiny

■ JOHN JUNG, CO-FOUNDER, ICF

On June 8, 2012, Riverside California, a thriving community of over 300,000 people east of Los Angeles, became the first North American city in five years and the first US city in a decade to receive ICF's coveted Intelligent Community of the Year Award. Upon accepting the award at Steiner Studios in Brooklyn, Mayor Ron Loveridge said, "I take immense pride in accepting the award for the most Intelligent Community in the world because it honors Riverside's excellence in so many of the key markers of success in the 21st century, including: high technology, workforce development, digital inclusion, arts, innovation, collaboration and social capital. We have been tested and assessed as world leaders and we are delighted to work with the ICF on spreading innovation throughout the global community." But it was not always so, and the road to success sometimes takes a bold move to take your own destiny in your hands to make it come true. This is the story of Riverside.

In the natural order of things, most living plants do not thrive in the shade of larger trees. However, some do, such as the Southern California Huckleberry (*Vaccinium ovatum*), which through evolution has learned to differentiate itself from other similar plants of its species and thrives accordingly.

Cities in the shadow of larger metropolitan areas also need to develop a way to differentiate themselves. It can't be artificial; it has to be true to itself; but it needs to be a unique brand or else it simply becomes engulfed into the metropolitan tsunami.

The Intelligent Community Forum has identified many such centers around the world that are in the shadow of great cities and yet are able to somehow thrive. Issy-les-Moulineaux is literally and figuratively in the shadow of the Eiffel Tower in Paris, but is its own strong intelligent community focused on its R&D base. Microsoft, Cisco and Orange research centers call Issy-les-Moulineaux home. Other examples are Whittlesea in greater Melbourne; Ipswich in the greater Brisbane area; Burlington, Stratford and Waterloo in the shadow of the greater Toronto region; Taichung City, Taoyuan and New Taipei City within the greater reaches of Taipei; Spokane nearby Seattle; Suwon and Gangnam within the greater Seoul area; Dublin in the shadow of Columbus, Ohio; and Mitaka within the Greater Tokyo environment. Each is establishing its own intelligent community focus and differentiating itself in various ways. These are also exceptional models for other centers around the world in the shadow or near-shadow of major metropolitan areas.

Likewise, Riverside, California is in the shadow of the seemingly never-ending reaches of Los Angeles. Just 42 miles from LAX Airport and about 60 miles from the center of the City of Los Angeles, Riverside has found a unique way to differentiate itself. So much so, that in 2012, the Intelligent Community Forum named Riverside as the Intelligent Community of the Year. Although a relatively small community in the shadow of one of the world's largest concentrations of humanity and creativity in Los Angeles,

Riverside today appears to be a thriving and upbeat center. But only about a dozen years ago it was known as merely a bedroom community in the shadow of LA and seen as a local center for logistics and warehousing, an agricultural hub and a university town. For many years it seemed to flounder and seemed incapable of retaining the knowledge base it was creating within its midst as many of the 55,000 students that attended the city's educational institutions every year left upon graduation to pursue their careers and lives elsewhere. Coupled with a large population of disadvantaged and struggling residents unfamiliar with computer technology and the economic downturn in 2004, the community felt a need to seek out new directions to leverage opportunities to harness the talent in the local institutions and develop and attract the high value tech sector in their community. In effect it needed a significant act of intervention to transform everything!

"We have been tested and assessed as world leaders and we are delighted to work with the ICF on spreading innovation throughout the global community."

Back in 1873, Mrs. Eliza Tibbets in Riverside seized her own destiny by introducing the first Parent Navel Orange tree from Bahia, Brazil, spawning California's entire citrus industry. This changed everything and transformed a dusty ranch community into a thriving citrus industry. Since navel oranges have no seeds, cuttings from the original trees were used to start navel orange groves throughout Southern California, and an incredible industry grew, making Riverside the wealthiest city in the United States at that time. Today, every navel orange grown in California is a descendant of this tree. Now that is taking your destiny in your own hands!

Similarly, more than a century later, Riverside needed to seize its own destiny by transforming everything that it seemed to be doing wrong. The turning point came when civic leaders undertook a visioning process that changed things in Riverside, forever. Mayor Ronald Loveridge and local institutional leaders convened a High Tech Taskforce, which ultimately evolved into the Riverside Technology CEO Forum, which still meets regularly today. This Taskforce sought to differentiate itself by attracting and creating high-tech firms in their community. Their strategy would be to generate, attract and retain the talent in the existing institutions in Riverside that would create and attract new high-paying jobs in the community. Their strategic effort called "Seizing our Destiny" formed around the idea to communicate, connect and measure. It would become a popular and well received community-driven campaign that built on the city's existing strengths to create a better place to live, work and play for future generations. The results included building a fiber network to connect the University Research Park and City's operations. It also created the office of the Chief Information Officer and Smart Riverside, and many more directions, meetings its 11 top strategic goals.

Building on these efforts, the University of California at Riverside and the City of Riverside partnered on several other initiatives, from incubators to web-based hubs involving educational social and community services, such as College 311, targeting opportunities to increase college degrees; a highly-acclaimed virtual secondary school; and an Innovation Center offering incubation space, business acceleration and interaction with angel and venture investors. Leveraging and collaboration are key ingredients to differentiating success in Riverside, which count several dozen new high-tech companies and tech start-ups as resulting from these recent actions.

As a result, this formerly poor and undereducated, underserviced bedroom community, has literally and figuratively transformed itself in little more than a decade to be nearly completely wireless, offering high speed internet choices, embracing fiber infrastructure, becoming a major research center, an outstanding source for high technology graduates, providing 24 hour "virtual city hall" access, implementing dozens of leading edge citizen centered applications, providing business and employee incentives, and is a model city for high technology collaboration. And it is making a name for itself regionally and abroad in the process, attracting new Foreign Direct Investments, including over $13 Million from Winston Global Energy in China, transforming the University of California at Riverside into a major research center for battery and clean energy research. Building on the heritage of Eliza Tippets - now that is taking your destiny in your own hands! ■

THE TOP7 OF 2012
Riverside, California, USA
Creating an innovation ecosystem from scratch

■ ROBERT BELL, CO-FOUNDER, ICF

By the year 2004, Riverside had just about run out of luck.

For more than a century, nature and circumstance had been kind to this city, 60 miles (96 km) inland from Los Angeles on the Santa Ana River in the foothills of the San Gabriel and San Bernadino Mountains. In 1874, a resident named Eliza Tibbets received two Brazilian navel orange trees from a friend at the US Department of Agriculture. They thrived in Southern California's climate – just in time for the development of refrigerated railroad cars and advanced irrigation. Within 20 years, Riverside was home to half of the citrus trees in California and had become the wealthiest city per capita in the United States.

The citrus economy throve in a location with vast amounts of agricultural land (once it was irrigated) and attracted a big workforce of manual laborers. It gave birth, in 1907, to the University of California Citrus Experiment Station, which became the University of California, Riverside (UCR). UCR pioneered research in biological pest control and growth regulators responsible for extending the citrus-growing season from four to nine months.

> **The 2012 Intelligent Community of the Year**

The wealth it created is still visible today in such architectural treasures as the Metropolitan Museum, Riverside Art Museum and the Mission Inn, which has been a holiday destination for no fewer than seven US Presidents of the United States.

Riverside In Brief

Population
306,800

Labor Force
160,700

Size
82 sq miles

Top Industries
Government, educational & health services, retail.

Broadband Penetration
79% households, 99% business, 100% government, 98% education.

Degrees Awarded
Community college 2,600; undergrad 4,080; graduate 990.

3-Year Job Creation
-6,600 (-6,000 net), 600 depending on ICT.

Key Leaders
Mayor Ronald Loveridge

Scott Barber, Interim City Manager

Steve Reneker, Chief Information Officer

Surrendering the Crown

But King Citrus could not reign forever. The Sixties and Seventies brought vast improvements in global transportation that transformed agriculture into a multinational business in which Riverside struggled to compete. As the citrus economy declined, Riverside's relatively cheap land and labor found new uses. The city became a warehouse and transit center supporting the nearby Ontario Airport, with more than 120 trains a day moving cargo through Riverside from the Port of Los Angeles. Education also expanded rapidly. Today, almost 20% of Riverside's population consists of students at UCR, California Baptist University, La Sierra University and Riverside City College.

The Eighties and Nineties brought more change. As housing prices soared in the Los Angeles Basin, Riverside's  lower-priced land once again proved a lure. Former Angelinos proved willing to endure 2-hour commutes for a chance to have a bigger home in a beautiful place. Electric and water rates that were 30% those of surrounding counties helped. These forces transformed Riverside into a bedroom community for Los Angeles. Meanwhile, about 10% of the population – providing manual labor in the fields and warehouses – remained poor, poorly educated and fertile ground for the gang culture that was spilling inland from the coast.

By the first decade of the 21st Century, Riverside was a community split into fragments. Its population was 49% Hispanic, 34% white, 7% Asian and 7% African-American. Police, fire, utility, and other government departments operated in silos. The city's information technology department – including the position of CIO – had been outsourced in the Nineties, which created an ideal opportunity for the outsourcer to maximize its own revenue at the city's expense. Population growth was rapidly outstripping the ability of the city to manage it. By 2004, resident satisfaction with city departments was at an all-time low. Smog and traffic were seen as severe problems. Police operations were in such disarray that the US Government had to intervene. And university graduates, diplomas in hand, quickly decamped for more promising locations.

Foundations of a New Economy
In 2004, Riverside Mayor Ron Loveridge and John Tillquist, Dean of Economic Development at Riverside Community College, convened a High Technology Taskforce to see if something could be done about getting a bigger share of California's tech-driven prosperity. The Taskforce included government and university leaders as well as CEOs from Riverside's small number of research-oriented tech companies. It spurred creation of a second group, the Riverside Technology CEO Forum, which became a place for business leaders to discuss their mutual concerns and formulate plans for action. Together, the groups solicited feedback from business, community groups, city department heads and university leaders. They produced a roadmap that would be familiar today to the leaders of any Intelligent Community. It focused on promoting technology businesses and creating the information infrastructure they needed, fostering entrepreneurship in higher education, improving the skills of the population and demanding that city government set an example of tech-based innovation for others to follow.

There is an old proverb saying that the road to hell is paved with good intentions. To avoid that fate, Mayor Loveridge and the City Council went looking for new administrative leadership to translate ideas into action.

In 2005, Riverside hired a new city manager, Brad Hudson, with long experience in economic development, and its first full-time CIO, Steve Reneker. A year later, the city hired Greg Lee to serve as a single point of contact for attracting and retaining high-tech businesses.

One thing that high-tech business demanded was high-speed, highly reliable connectivity. With its universities, transport businesses and affluent commuters, Riverside had proved attractive to telecom companies that deployed broadband in the 1990s. But a decade later, coverage was still limited, and it was obvious that carriers saw far more opportunity in the Los Angeles metro area to the west.

Riverside seized the opportunity to change that dynamic in 2007 by contracting with AT&T to deploy a city-wide WiFi network. It provided free 512 Kbps access to individual users (since raised to 1 Mbps), 1 Mbps access for city departments and a 4.9 GHz network for public safety. The network has 1,600 access points across Riverside's 55 square mile (142 km2) developed area. By 2010, AT&T exited the municipal wireless business and transferred ownership to the city, but the project had done its work. The WiFi network proved the strong demand in Riverside for broadband service, and carriers including AT&T, Verizon and Charter Cable began

> Businesses took the gamble because they saw a ready-made supply of entrepreneurial talent in the students at Riverside institutions.

to deploy 20-50 Mbps services throughout the city to supplement the wireless system.

Assembling the Ecosystem

The High Technology Taskforce and CEO Forum were not meant to be just talking shops. They were the core of collaborative teams that set out to assemble an innovation ecosystem for Riverside.

The new CIO, Steve Reneker, renegotiated the city's outsourcing contract to a "cost plus" formula, which saved more than $4 million. The city ploughed it back into refreshing its technology, building a fiber backbone to control city facilities and systems, and building a state-of-the-art network operations center. An advanced traffic management center now controls the complex flow of traffic and trains to eliminate bottlenecks. Average commute time through the city has been reduced by 30%.

His team implemented video security in parks and at railroad crossing, using cameras linked to the wireless network, and a Riverside Resident Connect system for reporting problems by phone, email, or submission of a photo taken with a smartphone. They also built from scratch an innovative graffiti abatement system connecting multiple departments. City workers take photos of graffiti with their smartphones and transmit them to the system, where pattern recognition software matches it to an ever-growing database of images. The system generates work orders for removal of the graffiti at the same time it supports preparation of criminal complaints by the City Attorney. Since its introduction, successful prosecutions have generated $200,000 in restitution for the city, and funded the removal of a lot of graffiti.

Business also did its part. Supporting the city's efforts, Riverside's tech companies began to set up their own incubators to spur innovation. ISCA, which uses electronic technologies to solve pest problems, began offering office space and production facilities to start-ups in 2008. In 2009, Bourns, a manufacturer of electronic components, established the second incubator. A maker of customer relationship management systems, Surado, included incubator space in its new Surado Corporate Center. And Avisio, a publicly traded technology innovation company, established an Innovation Economy Initiative to assist in the commercialization of emerging technologies.

Businesses took these gambles because they saw the ready-made supply of entrepreneurial talent represented by Riverside's 48,000 university and community college students. And the academic sector proved to be a willing partner in connecting classroom and laboratory innovation to opportunities in the marketplace. UC Riverside has become a leading research center for nanotechnology and solar energy. Riverside's first incubator, the Riverside Innovation Center, was created by the city and UC Riverside. Within three years of start-up, it became the headquarters of eight new high-tech companies. Surado and Avisio both got their start there, as did OmniPlatform, developer of online applications for emergency room management.

The Riverside Community College, with nearly 20,000 students, operates the Tritech Business Development Center. Using funding from the US Small Business Administration and local sponsors, TriTech provides free counseling, networking and workshops. Its counselors are successful local entrepreneurs in high-tech fields. Together with the Tech Coast Angels investor group, it has trained 270 potential entrepreneurs and established 20 technology start-ups. It also partners with the city, CEO Forum and universities to host an annual venture creation competition, The Big Idea, that awards cash prizes and in-kind services to students and start-up companies invited to pitch their product or idea to a group of investors.

Renewable Opportunity

In 2009, the city partnered with UC Riverside and its Bourns College of Engineering, as well as sister city Sendai, Japan and Sendai's Tohoku University, to launch the Southern California Research Initiative for Solar Energy (SC-RISE). In collaboration with Federal agencies, SC-RISE researches new solar technologies such as high-temperature solar thermal energy storage. It is testing and implementing new technologies like thin-film solar cells with researchers at Tohoku University and rare-earth yttrium batteries with Winston Global Energy in Shenzhen, China.

Winston Global Energy is partnering with Riverside's SolarMax Technology to build a 2 MW solar generation and storage project at UC Riverside, and is working with the city and Riverside Public Utilities to develop a 20 MW solar generation strategy for the city. SolarMax has joined forces with the city to create a renewable energy program that has won the right from the US government to offer up to 160 foreign nationals permanent US residency in exchange for investment of $500,000 in a Riverside business that creates at least 10 jobs. The program has generated $15 million already, focused on installation of rooftop solar systems, and expects to create 1,600 direct and indirect solar installation jobs in Riverside.

Riverside residents recognize the transformation that these many efforts have brought. In 2009, the Chamber of Commerce, City and UC Riverside sponsored a program to involve the entire community in establishing a vision of prosperity and a detailed roadmap to reach it, which was branded "Seizing our Destiny." In a recent survey, two thirds said they would continue to support the government's push for high-tech opportunities even if it meant higher taxes – this in the region that gave birth to America's taxpayer revolt of the 1980s.

The Next Generation

Riverside's leadership has also recognized that prosperity cannot simply be imported. Community leaders have formed groups including the Education Roundtable and Higher Education Business Council to focus on improving education and extending it to every segment of the community. They report regularly to City Council and document progress on the city's "Seizing our Destiny" Web site.

Dr. Rick Miller, superintendent of the Riverside Unified School District (RUSD), has committed his schools to getting technology into the hands of students. RUSD provides 10,000 electronic mobile devices and digital text books for students. RUSD's Ramona High School was the first in California to have all 2,100 students using digital (Coby Android) textbooks with wireless connectivity to teacher Web sites.

The Science and Technology Education Partnership (STEP) is a nonprofit organization established by the US Congressman for Riverside's district. Every October, 3,500 students from 30 schools attend STEP's science and technology conference at the Riverside Convention Center. It aims to ignite the imaginations of students about the exciting career opportunities available to students in science and technology, and to provide teachers with innovative ideas for math and science lessons. The program has reached 25,000 students and 2,000 teachers since its start in 1999.

In 2009, the Bill and Melinda Gates Foundation and the National League of Cities chose Riverside as one of four cities receiving $3.1 million to increase the number of young people age 16-26 who complete post-secondary education with value in the marketplace. Riverside used its grant to create Completion Counts, a Web-based public information hub offering educational, social and community services. Its goal is to double the number of Riverside students who complete college by 2020.

The Digital Learning Revolution

The Riverside Unified School District (RUSD) is the 15th largest in the state of California, but it leads in applying digital technologies to innovate in education.

In 2011, RUSD set out to create California's first all-digital secondary school at Riverside's Ramona High School. In a program called the Digital Learning Revolution, RUSD digitized all learning materials and made Android-based tablets available to every Ramona student. The district also encouraged those who wished to bring their own devices to school, and created the apps to run on them.

The RUSD app allowed student to take notes and highlight material in the content they read – something the district could never permit with hard-copy books. It also gave students access to video content, interactive apps and teachers' notes.

Such broad-based use of technology is impressive. But does it work? RUSD was one of four districts chosen to pilot the FUSE Algebra 1 app designed by Houghton Mifflin Harcourt for the Apple iPad. In a year-long study, students received instruction in two ways. One group was taught using only a textbook while the other group used the FUSE app, which included the textbook content, instructional videos and interactive programming that encouraged repeat practice. At the end of the year, students who worked with the FUSE app scored 20 percentage points higher on standardized tests than peers who used only textbooks.

The Digital Learning Revolution also brought new transparency to measuring each student's progress. RUSD introduced a Digital Dashboard, resembling the dashboard on a car, which gave students a near-real-time view of their progress, based on grades from each quiz, test or assignment. A bigger departure from standard American educational practice would be hard to find. Students no longer see just grades on individual assignments but a cumulative picture of where they stand. Families no longer have to wait until the end of the grading period to know how their kids are doing, and can catch problems early. It took something of a revolution in the school's back office to accomplish, but the results have justified RUSD's highest hopes. The Digital Dashboard also won the respect of Intelligent Community leaders attending ICF's 2012 Summit, who voted it winner of the Coolest Broadband App of the year.

Nearly 70% of RUSD students receive free or reduced lunch benefits – a marker of low incomes in the US – and many cannot afford the latest digital technology. RUSD worked aggressively to marshal funding from the US government and corporations for the program, while the SmartRiverside nonprofit also played a crucial role in providing refurbished computers, training and WiFi access to families in need. As a result, RUSD has put nearly 20,000 digital devices into the hands of students throughout the district and given nearly half of RUSD students a helping hand into the broadband economy.

SmartRiverside and Digital Inclusion

The final component of the innovation ecosystem in Riverside focuses on those who have been left out. Digital inclusion is a top priority for the Mayor and Council, and implementation is the responsibility of an organization called SmartRiverside. It is headed by CIO Steve Reneker.

SmartRiverside operates a Digital Inclusion Center that gets technology and training into the hands of the excluded. The technology comes from a unique collaboration between a computer services company that collects e-waste, and a gang prevention program called Project Bridge. The company hires and trains former gang members recruited by Project Bridge to refurbish the used PCs. Equipment that cannot be refurbished is sold to a certified local recycler. Working equipment other than PCs is refurbished and sold on eBay, and these sources of revenue help pay for the program.

SmartRiverside provides the refurbished computers to school districts in the region for computer labs, as well as directly to 200 new low-income families per month. After school hours, teachers provide certified computer training in the labs to families at no or low cost. SmartRiverside also partners with Riverside County and The Salvation Army, a faith-based social service organization, to offer free technology training, Internet access and PCs to low-income seniors. Add to this the 3,500 hours of computer time amassed by residents each month at Riverside's Eastside Cybrary (a library without books), and Riverside is clearly on the leading edge in digital inclusion.

The financial crisis that began in 2008 cruelly revealed the weaknesses of the bedroom community model that came to dominate Riverside's economy in the Eighties and Nineties. The housing market collapse hit Riverside doubly hard because so many of its residents were employed in housing construction and development. Many people lost their homes as the city experienced one of the highest home foreclosure rates in the United States. In the recession, Riverside's unemployment rate exceeded 14%, one in seventeen homes were in foreclosure and property values dropped back to 1999 levels. For the city, property tax revenues declined 40% in 2009 alone.

But at the same time, Riverside has continued to invest in a five-year, $1.6 billion "Riverside Renaissance" program. That investment has gone into improving traffic flows, replacing aging water, sewer and electric infrastructure and expanding and improving police, fire and other community services. It is a physical manifestation of the social and economic changes that the community has put into motion. It is also a vote of confidence in the future for a community that has seized its destiny and is not looking back. ■

PLATFORMS FOR INNOVATION
Lessons from Intelligent Communities

Targeting Small Business Development
Dublin, Ohio, USA
Top7 Intelligent Community 2010-2011

Dublin is a suburb of Columbus, the state capital of Ohio, known for its DubLink community network, which has boosted broadband competition while making possible a rich array of online government services. Dublin does much more to build its economy, however, than just transport information. The city is a partner of TechColumbus, a regional nonprofit whose mission is to accelerate the growth of the innovation economy through business plan counseling, market assessment and help in gaining access to capital. More than 60 Dublin companies have benefited to date. The $625,000 that the city invested in TechColumbus in 2009 has already yielded $14.6 million in investment, debt financing and new revenue.

The city's Dublin Entrepreneurial Center (DEC) opened in 2009 with one start-up tenant and now houses nearly 50 companies and support organizations, including the Center for Innovative Food Technology and the Ohio Fuel Cell Coalition. It hosts twice-monthly co-working events, where Dublin's business community participates in training and meets the community's newest entrepreneurial class. Inspired by its participation in ICF's programs, the city is also establishing a Center for Global Business Development at DEC to provide collaboration, education and support for Dublin companies seeking to do business overseas.

This ongoing effort to support and strengthen entrepreneurship helps explain why there are 3,000 companies in Dublin, with an average of just seven employees each, while the city is also home to multinational corporations such as Wendy's International and Ashland.

> The mission of TechColumbus is to accelerate the growth of the innovation economy.

Innovative young companies include Neoprobe, which develops biomedical devices to improve cancer surgery outcomes; EnergyGateway, which offers energy management services to commercial customers and was recently acquired by WorldEnergy; Sypherlink, whose software automates data-sharing across the enterprise; and Cardiox, which sells detection systems for the prevention of strokes. ■

Investing in the Growth of SMEs
Suwon, South Korea
Intelligent Community of the Year 2010

City government allocates US$27m per year as investment capital to strengthen the competiveness of SMEs. The funding is designed to be matched by private investment or bank loans, but for companies too small to attract private financing, Suwon offers subsidies of up to $18,000 to support prototype development. Suwon also has an innovative Electronic Trade Office (www.tradr.go.kr) that connects to other Korean cities as well as partner cities in Asia, Europe and Latin America. The Office offers products online for sale by

Suwon companies and provides a videoconferencing system to promote deal-making without the need to travel. To date, companies have sold $200,000 worth of products through the Office. A branch office of the Korean Trade Investment Promotion Agency extends this effort by providing overseas representation for Suwon companies. From 2003 to 2008, nearly 500 local businesses took part in expositions and market development projects.

Anyone with experience in municipal government knows that just throwing money at a problem is no guarantee of success. While betting taxpayers' money on programs and companies, Suwon has also built a web of collaborative relationships among industry, universities and government. The tangible result is a large number of public-private research centers and institutes, including the Gyeonggi Regional Research Center, Content Convergence Software Research Center, Gyeonggi Bio Center, Korea Nano Fab Center, Next Generation Convergence Technology Institute and Green Energy, Auto Parts & Material Research Center. Some are located at local institutions including Sungkyunkwan University and Gyeonggi University. Others are based in yet another development, Kwangkyo Techno Valley, a $450m campus that is home to 145 R&D organizations.

> Two-thirds of Suwon companies specialize in one of its targeted industries, and companies with 50 or fewer employees make up 94% of all employers in the city.

Seven years of nurturing SMEs in specific industries have borne fruit. Two-thirds of Suwon companies specialize in one of its targeted industries: electronics, medical devices, chemicals and specialty metals. Companies with 50 or fewer employees make up 94% of all employers in the city. ■

THE TOP7 OF 2012
Saint John, New Brunswick, Canada
A city in distress builds a collaborative future

■ ROBERT BELL, CO-FOUNDER, ICF

In 2000, when the rest of the the planet was celebrating the turn of the century, the city of Saint John was in mourning. It grieved for the passing of a 20-year period of prosperity built on heavy industry and natural resources.

It was in the millenium year that Saint John Shipbuilding completed work on a program to build nine warships for the Canadian Navy, which had provided high-paying jobs for the skilled trades and attracted much private capital investment. With no new contracts on the horizon, the shipyard closed. In the same year, Lantic Sugar – a fixture of the local economy since 1915 – closed its refinery to centralize operations in Montreal.

Saint John stands at the mouth of the St. John River as it flows into the Bay of Fundy on the Atlantic coast, and as long served as the port through which the natural abundance of New Brunswick province flows. The impact of these two closings on the harbor city was severe. Retailers closed shop and home prices fell. Commercial buildings abandoned by their owners fell into disrepair. The population fell as people, many of them the community's best and brightest, moved on in search of work. Employment in manufacturing plummeted 26% from 1989 to 2003. And the shredding of the economy made visible a problem that had long lain in the shadows: more than one-quarter of Saint John's people lived below the poverty line and had been there for decades. Sixty percent of single parents in Saint John were poor, the vast majority young women who, more than likely, had been raised by a single mother themselves. Poverty in Saint John wore a woman's face.

If the crisis came abruptly, it had also been long in the making. The shipyard had only to check a calendar to know when the Navy program would run out. But a combination of Canadian government policy and the aggressive growth of Asian shipyards reduced its competitiveness in global markets. Liberalization of global trade also brought fierce new competition from low-cost countries for the commodities produced by the province of New Brunswick. The signs were there for those who cared to look but it took a crisis to shock the community into action.

Hidden Jewels

Fortunately, Saint John entered the new century with some valuable assets hidden in plain sight. Since the 1980s, the provincial telephone company, NBTel, had pursued a unique strategy. Foreseeing that liberalization would eventually end its monopoly, the company decided to fortify its competitive position by deploying fiber-optic infrastructure and was the first in Canada to introduce new services from voicemail and caller ID to Internet access. The first customers were big business, major institutions and government offices across the province – but NBTel also created an Emerging Business Group to develop specialized services. Its original focus was in the development of electronic patient records and teleradiology for the health and life sciences sector. The company went on to create its own stable of start-up companies to provide computer-telephone integration to customers and streaming video over telephone wires.

Despite these advances, when the telecom market opened, a Saint John entrepreneur, Bill Stanley, decided to move his cable TV company into telephone services and launched a fiber overbuild across the province. Saint John found itself the early beneficiery of a competitive shootout between telecom providers.

In addition to infrastructure, the community had the core of a knowledge economy. Aggressive lobbying by Saint John had led the University of New Brunswick to open a campus there in 1964. Since welcoming its first class of 100, UNB Saint John went on to create Canada's first computer science department and e-commerce program, while growing its enrollment to 2,500 students. Over the decades, it educated thousands of local residents, many of them first-generation university graduates, and most went on to work for and lead local companies.

The community had one more asset that would prove crucial in the coming decade: entrepreneurial talent. The best known was K.C. Irving, who opened a gas station and car dealership in 1925 and died in 1992 as one of Canada's richest men, with an estimated net work of C$6 billion. His Irving Oil is now a leading refiner and marketer of petroleum products in northeastern North America, and its Saint John refinery is the largest in Canada.

Saint John also had Gerry Pond. He was the last CEO of NBTel, which was merged into four other regional telcos by their corporate parent, Bell Canada, to form Aliant.

Saint John In Brief

Population
68,000

Labor Force
35,615

Size
315 km²

Top Industries
Healthcare and social assistance, retail, administrative and support, manufacturing, construction.

Broadband Penetration
75% households, 90% businesses, 100% government, 100% educational & nonprofit.

Degrees Awarded
Community college 645; undergrad 425; graduate 81.

3-Year Job Creation
3,500 (2,300 net), 600 depending on ICT.

Key Leaders
Steve Carson, CEO, Enterprise Saint John

Gerry Pond, Senior Partner, Mariner Partners

Monica Chaperlin, Coordinator, Business Community Anti-Poverty Initiative

After watching the new organization disperse the innovative teams he had built from scratch, Mr. Pond retired from the company in 2001. But neither he nor the ICT entrepreneurs he had mentored were finished contributing to Saint John.

The Just-Right Community
A small city like Saint John has certain advantages that big municipalities can only envy. It is big enough to have the infrastructure of a modern city but small enough to have an intimate network of community leaders. In Saint John in particular, that network prides itself on collaboration. These advantages proved powerful as Saint John responded to crisis.

By 2003, the municipal councils of Saint John and four surrounding towns had agreed on a coordinated development strategy and tasked the economic development agency, Enterprise Saint John (ESJ), with implementing it. The strategy, called True Growth, aimed to harness business, institutions and three levels of government to jointly focus on development of sectors including ICT, life sciences, tourism, energy and advanced manufacturing.

Local government did its part. It made investments in e-government including an analytics platform for the police department, modeled on New York Ciy's CompStat, that gave managers timely intelligence on areas where crimes were most likely to occur. In its first year of operation, the police force achieved a 27% decrease in breaking-and-entering and an 18% decrease in motor vehicle thefts. A Municipal Energy Efficiency Program tracked energy consumption using technology from a Saint John company, and replaced equipment with more efficient models. Since 1998, the program has reduced consumption by 15% and generated annual savings for the city of C$1.7 million.

Enterprise Saint John worked with employers to identify needs, recruit skilled workers and strengthen company human resource practices through labor market research, recruitment campaigns and job fairs. It created an Emerging Entrepreneurs Program to educate young people on starting their own businesses and matched them with mentors, entirely through Facebook and Twitter. An Arts Entrepreneur Program focuses specifically onhe needs of artists and producers in crafts, literary arts, music, performing and visual arts.

ESJ's most recent effort is the Business Immigrant Mentorship Program, which provides immigrant entepreneurs with the chance to network with local business people. The program has been a success because of the eagerness of local business people to engage, from business training to one-on-one mentoring. Newcomers learn how to set up a business while they are establishing their first professional network; mentors gain insight into business and cultural practice in other parts of the world.

Saint John is also skilled at helping business tap provincial and regional funding programs. The National Research Council opened an e-health office in Saint John in 2002 to advance R&D in the field. The Atlantic Innovation Fund provides grants to universities, institutes and businesses for research into technology-based products or services with commercial potential. The New Brunswick Innovation Foundation has a similar mission but extends it to support for business starts as well.

As a publicly-funded university, UNB Saint John has a mission to conribute to the community's growth. Rejecting the ivory tower academic model, it develops joint programming with the New Brunswick Community College in Saint John and Dalhousie University to equip a wide range of students with the skills needed by a new generation of companies. The university houses a state-of-the-art distance learning center for Dalhousie's medical school and the community college's Allied Health Building, which provides training for medical technicians. The Saint John campus also uses UNB's alumni network to recruit students from Asia, the Middle East and Europe, bringing essential talent into the community.

Since its founding, UNB Saint John has launched research institutes linked to emerging economic sectors in the region. The Integrated Multi-Trophic Aquaculture Systems Group researches the cultivation of fish, shellfish and seaweed, and was instrumental in establishing an aquaculture industry in the Bay of Fundy. The university's intellectual property policy vests ownership in the faculty members and students who create it, rather than seeking to generate royalty income for the university. This kind of policy has been instrumental in the success of Canadian technology leaders like Waterloo, Ontario, the 2007 Intelligent Community of the Year.

Propelling Innovation

But few organizations have had the impact of Mariner Partners, founded by former NBTel CEO Gerry Pond and a group of his staff. The company was created to consult on IPTV – one of the technologies to emerge from NBTel – but has had a transformative impact on Saint John as a mentor of ICT startups. In 2004, Mariner Partners brought together its peers in Saint John's ICT sector to found PropelICT, a tech incubator with a difference. The founders saw no need for an organization that provided cheap office space. They believed that angel financing was available in the region for the right ideas. The missing link was mentorship. PropelICT reached into Saint John's collaborative business community and matched young entrepreneurs with senior business executives.

In its first three years, PropelICT nurtured 21 start-ups. Successes included Brovada, a market leader in business software for the insurance industry; SHIFT Energy, which provides real-time energy use analysis; and DealerMine, a relationship-management platform for car dealers.

PropelICT launched in 2006 the first Angel Investor Summit in Atlantic Canada, and created an group of in-kind angel investors – lawyers, accountants and other business service providers who provided free service to entrepreneurial companies in exchange for a small stipend from PropelICT and the hope that some would grow into much larger companies with substantial needs.

> Royal Bank vice president Bill Gale looked into the face of poverty in Saint John and decided to do something about it.

In 2007, the four founding employees of a new company called Radian6 joined Propell's accelerator program to develop a technology for monitoring social media engagement across all platforms. In March 2011, it was purchased for US$316 million by Salesforce.com, the leader in cloud-based customer relationship management systems, which announced at the same time that it would leave Radian6, with its 400+ employees, right where it was.

While accomplishing all this, Mariner Partners also developed and launched two successful products that help telephone companies deliver IPTV. And the seeds of entrepreneurship planted by PropelICT began to take root throughout the community. A company called Innovatia introduced a patented system for simplifying the task of creating and maintaining asset-level standard operating procedures in complex industrial environments. It was developed after Irving Oil came to Innovatia for help in managing its own operations. Aquila Tours, a local tour organizer, has opened a Center for Cruise Excellence based on its own internal skills and knowledge development efforts, and introduced an online training and certification program in multiple languages.

Helping to boost the appetite for innovation has been #livelifeuptown, the hashtag for a campaign promoting the cool lifestyle of Uptown Saint John. More than 1,400 registered members use it for recommendations on where to eat, what do do and who to meet. It is citizen-led, much like another organization called Fusion, which formed in 2004 to be a catalyst for attracting and retaining young professionals. Its social mixers, called Parties with a Purpose, attract both young professionals and senior business and political leaders, and ties them to city's thriving art scene.

But innovation in Saint John is not all high-tech glamor. The Saint John Community Loan Fund is Canada's first microcredit community investment group. Its first-ever loan went to a man who wanted to start a business salvaging sunken logs from the bottom of a river. He was succcessful enough to repay the loan and obtain a second one for a new business venture. To date, the fund has disbursed over C$200,000 in loans, with an average value of $1,250, and has generated over C$3 million in new income for the community.

A Smarter Fight Against Poverty

One day in 1998, Royal Bank vice president Bill Gale looked into the face of poverty in Saint John and decided to do something about it. A man approached him for spare change – no unusual thing. But on that day, for some reason, Mr. Gale did more than dig into his pocket. He asked the man his story.

He was a roofer who had been injured, had run through his employment insurance and was now on welfare. He was trying to get by on about C$10 per day. Mr. Gale was appalled. He began calling people to confirm the man's story and learn the dimensions of poverty in his city. He convinced 35 friends and colleagues to attend a workshop, where they listened to their fellow Saint Johners describe what it was like to be poor in the city they shared.

It was the beginning of a volunteer organization called the Business Community Anti-Poverty Initiative (BCAPI). It began work by retaining Deloitte & Touche to undertake a study, funded by Irving Oil, of the best practices in poverty reduction. The study had two major conclusions: children of single parents living in poverty were the group most at risk to be poor themselves, and the most effective way to help them was ensure they received a high school diploma.

Using the report's conclusions as its roadmap, BCAPI has worked ever since to make poverty reduction a community priority and to increase opportunities for poor children, youth and single parents. It engages, not in direct action, but by employing the business skills of its members to make community groups more effective and conducting research to measure that effectiveness.

BCAPI currently supports five community organizations, from First Steps, a safe haven for homeless mothers that helps them move to self-sufficiency, to the Resource Center for Youth, which offers teenagers recreation, self-development, health and wellness services, and help with school studies and employment. The Partners

Assisting Local Schools (PALS) program was created by J.K. Irving based on his involvement in BCAPI. It sends Irving Oil employees into schools to provide one-on-one mentoring for low-income students and funds educational technology. PALS received a Global Best award from the International Partnership Network, which celebrates outstanding community partnerships.

In the last three years, Saint John has seen net growth in jobs while the rest of New Brunswick – with the exception of 2010 Top7 community Moncton – has watched employment decline. Saint John is now home to more than 40 ICT companies as well as a thriving health and life sciences cluster in Tucker Park, where the university and Saint John Regional Hospital are located. Heavy industry remains part of the economic landscape: Canada's first liquified natural gas terminal began operation in Saint John's harbor in 2009. And in October 2011, Irving Shipbuilding announced a C$25 billion, 30-year contract with the Canadian navy. The vessels will be built in Halifax, in the province of Nova Scotia, but Saint John companies will provide components and services. When that contract runs out in 2041, it is likely to leave in its wake – not a crisis – but a community with a diverse, globally competitive economy that has found new ways to share the wealth with all of its citizens. ∎

PLATFORMS FOR INNOVATION
More Lessons from Intelligent Communities

Creating an Entrepreneurial Economy
Ottawa, Ontario, Canada
Top7 Intelligent Community 2007, 2010

Working in close collaboration with its educational institutions, Ottawa has built an infrastructure that develops talent, nurtures start-ups and connects them to opportunity. At the center of this effort is InvestOttawa, an economic development nonprofit funded by government and more than 700 member companies, which fosters the advancement of the region's knowledge-based institutions and industries. InvestOttawa's goal is strikingly simple: to make Ottawa recognized as one of the most innovative cities worldwide. It acts as a catalyst and contributor for government, university and private programs reaching from research labs and incubators to school classrooms.

TalentBridge is an InvestOttawa program that provides entrepreneurially-inclined university students with government-funded part-time jobs, working under experienced mentors, at local technology companies. The companies get the benefit of fresh thinking and new energy, while students gain business experience and often make the move into full-time positions with the companies.

Ottawa serial entrepreneur Terry Matthews has created the Wesley Clover Affiliate Program, named for his investment firm. Wesley Clover works with local universities to identify the brightest and most motivated new graduates, puts them through a "boot camp" training program for 9-12 months, and then pairs them with industry leaders in specific vertical segments. The aim is to introduce a new product into the market within 12 months of team formation. Since 2007, the program has incorporated seven new companies, of which four are generating revenue and two are undergoing a "friends and family" round of investment.

> 'Lead to Win' identifies seasoned managers of technology companies helps them launch new tech-based businesses.

InvestOttawa's Business Accelerator targets high-potential companies and offers them coaching, market analysis, support services, and access to OCRI's global network of investors for six months to a year. It aims to help young companies shift into high gear through market entry and financing. When they do, they can also take advantage of InvestOttawa Global Marketing, which maintains relationships with Canada's representatives throughout the world. A recent 2-day program took ambassadors and high commissioners who represent their countries in the Canadian capital on a tour of Ottawa's technology clusters, which resulted in new export business for participating companies.

Lead to Win identifies seasoned managers of technology companies who have been turfed out by corporate downsizing and helps them launch new technology-based businesses. The program originated in 2002 during the telecom recession and was revived when the latest downturn struck in

2008. Applicants accepted into the program receive training on business ecosystems, entrepreneurial management, and success factors for start-up tech companies. Those who start businesses are connected to strategic customers, sales opportunities and resources including financing. Out of the 61 participants in 2009, over 60% launched businesses. It is too soon to know how they will fare, but the businesses launched by the class of 2002 have created over 300 jobs and attracted more than C$90m in investment.

Ottawa's success in technology has yet to produce a substantial private venture capital sector ready to fund start-up and early-stage companies. National and provincial programs fill some of the gap. Ontario Centers of Excellence offer up to C$250,000 for market readiness and proof-of-concept programs. An Investment Accelerator Fund offers investments of up to C$500,000 to help launch high-potential technology ventures. The Emerging Technologies Fund matches private-sector investment up to C$5 million in early-stage companies, while the Next Generation Jobs Fund supports R&D and commercialization in new industries such as cleantech, biotech, ICT and digital media. ■

How Higher Education Drives Innovation
Windsor-Essex, Ontario, Canada
Top7 Intelligent Community 2010-2011

Windsor is the Canadian half of the automotive manufacturing zone it shares with Detroit, on the US side of the border. The University of Windsor, with nearly 16,000 students has long conducted research for auto manufacturers and hosted a multi-school R&D program called Auto21. But under President Alan Wildeman, appointed in 2008, UWindsor has sharply raised its game as a generator of economic value.

An Institute for Diagnostic Imaging Research (IDIR) does pioneering work in the uses of ultrasound for testing. The Institute has developed a way to use ultrasound for fingerprint recognition that detects tissue patterns beneath the skin as well as the conventional fingertip whorls. It is now ready for commercial development and the University, which allows inventors to retain the rights to intellectual property they create, is helping to find the right commercial partners. In another lab, scientists have solved the problem of testing spot-welds made between two pieces of flat metal. Because the welds themselves are hidden by the metal, they have traditionally been tested by pulling random samples off the assembly line and tearing them apart. The new system is already on the line at a Chrysler assembly plant in Windsor and has given a significant boost to quality and productivity.

> Graduates of the MediaPlex learn not just conventional journalism but also how to produce TV and radio news, write blogs and use social media.

The university is now in the midst of the largest capital expansion in its history. The centerpiece is a C$112 million Center for Engineering Innovation. In addition to labs and classrooms, it provides collocation facilities where companies can install industrial equipment and trouble-shoot problems and pioneer new techniques. It will house the university's Center for Smart Community Innovation, a group that has played an essential role in coordinating Intelligent Community initiatives among 54 participating organizations. President Wildeman envisions the new building as an innovation destination in eastern Canada for academia and industry.

UWindsor is not the only academic institution seeking to build a stronger future. St. Clair College is a 2-year institution that serves over 7,000 students in Windsor. Among its recent innovations is the MediaPlex. Opening in 2010, the building is one of only three places in the world that teach "convergence journalism." Graduates of the MediaPlex program learn not just conventional journalism but also how to record, edit and produce finished TV and radio news, write blogs and use social media for reporting. Despite the shrinking job market for journalists, students with this "backpack journalism" training find themselves in high demand. Overall, 82% of St. Clair graduates find employment within six months. ■

Government-Business-University Innovation Triangle
Arlington County, Virginia, USA
Top7 Intelligent Community 2010

From broadband to e-government and from education to economic development, Arlington has planned for continued prosperity. An important part of that plan was put into place in 2004, when a study by Arlington Economic Development identified the "government-industry-university innovation triangle" as fundamental to the county's economy. Close linkages among government agencies, key industry sectors and academic institutions form the triangle. Government research contracts fund local high-tech research at universities, which contribute to spin-offs of new companies whose products and services contribute to the success of the Federal government.

The county's innovation triangle is represented by such firms as GridPoint, a leader in software that helps utilities manage the complex web of devices and networks that will bring about the smart grid. FortiusOne, a venture-backed company founded by a former professor at George Mason University, provides real-time dynamic geospatial information to business and government, helping them to better visualize and share map-based data. These are just a few of the companies located in high-tech zones established by the county. The zones provide reduced business license tax rates as an incentive.

> Close linkages among government agencies, key industry sectors and academic institutions form the triangle.

But a more powerful incentive is Arlington's natural advantage as a lower-cost location next to Washington DC, with fast, reliable transit to the urban core. The Commonwealth of Virginia also offers incentive programs to promote start-ups, connect small business to business opportunities with Federal and corporate buyers, and fund scientific research with commercial potential.

Innovation takes brain power, and the county has used this concept in successful efforts to save jobs threatened by changes in Federal policy. In 2004, Arlington was threatened with the loss of Defense Department (DoD) employees occupying 4 million square feet of office space. Arlington developed a "Save the Brains" campaign targeted at the commission tasked with producing a list of facilities to close. In testimony and town-hall-style meetings, through buttons and bumper stickers, public relations and transit advertising, Arlington argued that clustering of DoD offices and the

National Science Foundation in the county contributed in major ways to DoD operations. The "Save the Brains" campaign not only saved the local jobs but gained media attention across the United States, contributing to Arlington's reputation as an innovation center. ■

THE TOP7 OF 2012
Stratford, Ontario, Canada
Leveraging a history of reinvention

■ ROBERT BELL, CO-FOUNDER, ICF

In the life of a community there are turning points, when events and decisions shape the future for generations to come. The small city of Stratford reached such a turning point in 1958.

The biggest employer in Stratford and the engine of its economy at that time was the steam locomotive maintenance yard of the Canadian National (CN) railroad. Times had never been better for the yard than they were in the early Sixties. CN was in the process of converting its steam locomotives to diesel and had concentrated all of its remaining steam engine maintenance work in Stratford, while assuring its employees that they would have an important part in maintaining the diesel locomotives of the future.

In 1958, the president of CN, who was on the Board of Stratford's leading cultural institution, the Shakespeare Festival, brought the bad news to town himself. Because diesel engines required less maintenance and ran longer before needing service, the company had decided to reduce the number of maintenance yards. Stratford was off the list. By

1964, the yard was closed, thousands of highly skilled employees lost their jobs, and the city's economy developed a massive hole, symbolized by the abandoned plant in the city center.

Stratford In Brief

Population
32,000

Labor Force
18,000

Size
25 km²

Top Industries
Manufacturing, healthcare & social services, education, business services, retail trade.

Broadband Penetration
100% households, 100% businesses, 100% government, 100% educational & nonprofit.

Degrees Awarded
N/A. Future degrees expected.

3-Year Job Creation
-1,600 (-900 net), +600 depending on ICT.

Key Leaders

Mayor Dan Mathieson

Doug MacDougald, President & CEO, South West Ontario Veterinary Services

Tobi Day Hamilton, Director, Advancement & Public Affairs, University of Waterloo Stratford

In response, a group of local businessmen created a volunteer group they grandly called the Stratford Industrial

Commission. They went to the City Council with an offer and a demand. They offered to scour North America for manufacturing companies that could be enticed to open a facility in Stratford and soak up its surplus skilled labor. In return, they wanted the right to make whatever deal they thought was in the city's best interest, without being second-guessed by Council.

The Council was in no mood to say 'no,' and the Commission members went to work chasing smokestacks with great success. The companies they attracted to Stratford gave the community several more decades of life as a low-cost, skilled manufacturing center.

This was not the first industrial transition the city had endured. Nor would it be the last. In the years following the Second World War, it had become home to businesses that manufactured one-sixth of all Canadian furniture, only to lose their economic advantage to lower-cost competitors. But Stratford's history of repeated rise and fall had equipped the community with the skills to reinvent itself under pressure. Those skills grew rusty at times but, like money in the bank, they were they there to be called upon when needed.

Shakespeare in the Park

Twelve years before CN closed the Stratford yard, a local journalist named Tom Patterson went to City Council with an idea. Stratford had beautiful parkland running along the Avon River and he thought the city should start a summer Shakespeare Festival there. Patterson volunteered to go to New York City and try to convince a director and actors to help found it. He asked for $100 to pay for his trip. As far-fetched as the idea sounded, the Council deliberated and then gave him $125. New York, after all, was an expensive place to visit.

It took more than one trip and a fair amount of faith on the part of Mr. Patterson and the Council. But the Stratford Shakespeare Festival opened in the park under a tent in the summer of 1953 with a production of *Richard III* directed by Tyrone Guthrie and starring Alec Guinness. It was so successful that, within a few years, the city commissioned a permanent theatre building to house it. When the project ran out of money, the general contractor, Oliver Gaffney, offered to finish the building at his own expense in return for a promissory note from the Festival. His act of faith paid off. Today, his daughter, Anita Gaffney, is the Administrative Director of a Festival that has become the community's largest employer, generating C$135 million in local economic activity and C$70 million in tax revenue for all levels of government.

By 2000, Stratford had a 3-sided economy. The manufacturing cluster has moved into automotive parts, which had become a major industry in southern Ontario Province. Farming is also a major industry. Lying between three of North America's Great Lakes, Stratford is at the center of the most productive agricultural land in Canada. The Festival, which employs 1,000 people during the summer season, forms the third side.

A three-sided structure should be stable, but by the end of the 20th Century, Stratford's leaders feared it would not carry the community forward. It was clear that US automobile manufacturing was in decline – a judgment validated in 2009 when the near-collapse of the industry caused another wave of job losses. Farming employed a tiny sliver of the population with little chance for employment growth. And the Festival, for all of the money and prestige it brought to Stratford, was a seasonal tourist business, which for most of the year employed fewer than 300 people.

With the metropolis of Toronto only two hours down the road, Stratford suffered a perennial brain drain of its best and brightest young people. The experience of nearby Waterloo – ICF's 2007 Intelligent Community of the Year – also dramatized how important information and communications technology could be to a local economy of the 21st Century. But Stratford was not equipped to play that game. It did not even have a seat at the table.

Community Vision 2010

In 1997, Stratford undertook a public consultation, gap analysis and visioning exercise to explore its future. Hundreds of residents and community leaders took part. The result was Community Vision 2010, which set that year as a deadline to transform the city's economy.

Before the vision could be achieved, however, Stratford needed to overcome its own acknowledged inertia and create ways to put Community Vision 2010 into action. In 2002, Council member and Deputy Mayor Dan Mathieson ran for Mayor. Elected in 2003, he brought his considerable energy and imagination to the task of leading Stratford into another round of reinvention, with the strong support of Council, city staff and a newly engaged citizenry.

> Stratford now had the digital infrastructure of a major metropolitan area, and its impact spread across the community.

Like many rural cities, Stratford owned its own municipal electric utility. In the 1990s, the utility had laid optical fiber along its rights of way to provide communications capacity for lease to large industrial customers. Then the

Province of Ontario began pushing cities to privatize their utilities. Refusing to give up local control of infrastructure, the Council chose a different path. It spun the utility off into a pair of private companies with the city as sole shareholder: Festival Hydro to own and operate the electrical system and Festival Hydro Services to become a data utility operating the dark fiber.

In 2012, the data utility was rebranded Rhyzome Networks and expanded its fiber network by 50% to 60 km (37 mi), while introducing up to 1 Gbps connections to 125 locations including city facilities and schools. Rhyzome also built a 300-hub WiFi network using fiber as the backbone. The anchor tenant was Festival Hydro, which used the fiber/WiFi platform roll out a smart meter program to its 18,000 customers in the region. Rhyzome originally retained the utility business model: it provide telecom services to city-owned facilities but leased dark fiber to commercial ISPs and local cooperatives serving the Shakespeare Festival and other business customers. In 2011, Rhyzome began providing its own ISP services to commercial and residential customers at up to 100 Mbps at half the price of incumbents.

Digital Assets of a Major Metropolis

Stratford now had the digital infrastructure of a major metropolitan area, and its impact spread across the community. The Festival had struggled for years with a 4 Mbps broadband connection that caused its content-rich Web site and online sales engine to freeze up. Switching to Rhyzome gave it 10 Mbps burstable to 100 Mbps on demand.

Stratford is the center of a four-hospital regional partnership called the Huron-Perth Health Alliance. It leases fiber from Rhyzome and other providers that connects 85%

of the physicians groups and family doctors in the Stratford area. The network allows centralized laboratories and specialized care units to serve a widely dispersed set of hospitals, clinics and medical practices, which saves time and money while delivering the highest possible quality of care to a largely rural area. Stratford General Hospital currently conducts 70,000 tests per year for patients in surrounding counties. Physically linked by twice-daily courier, lab results are turned around in hours and, for connected facilities, are available instantly. The interpretation of medical images is likewise centralized, so that four radiologists at Stratford General can serve the entire region – with another radiologist in Austria available for off-hours service.

Telemedicine projects include service for mental and emotional conditions that would otherwise need hospitalization. Staff is able to visit clients through a high-quality videoconference to check on their state of mind, ensure they are taking medications and consult on their issues. Client response is overwhelmingly positive: clients see the videoconference terminal not as Big Brother invading their homes but as a tangible sign they are being cared for. Caregivers are equally enthusiastic because eliminating travel time means they can spend more time with clients.

One goal of Community Vision 2010 was to expand Stratford's tourism industry to all four seasons. (Seasonal it might be, but tourism still generates $183 million per year in economic activity.) City Council and the local business community created a public-private Stratford Tourism Alliance and charged it with making that vision reality. The Alliance launched online and traditional advertising campaigns to make Stratford a destination for "foodies" and cultural tourists. From 2009 to 2010, the Alliance's Web traffic grew 200% while Ontario Tourism's traffic fell 18% in response to economic doldrums in the United States. More than half of all leisure travelers carry smartphones, and the Alliance introduced a mobile site in 2010 and mobile versions of its "Savor Stratford" foodies and Festival campaigns. Apps for the iPhone, iPad, Android and BlackBerry followed in 2011, which provided everything from reservations for hotels and restaurants to schedules of events and augmented reality. A set of walking tours of Stratford's many heritage buildings uses signs with QR codes to play 2-3 minute audio clips describing the history of each location.

Broadband infrastructure also played an important role in a decision by the Royal Bank of Canada (RBC) to locate one of its critical data centers in Stratford. Winning the facility was an uphill fight all the way for the small city. When leaders got wind of the opportunity, they had to push hard to be included on the list of potential sites. But Mayor Mathieson and the economic development team believed the time was right. The city had recently invested $5.3 million in creating a pre-zoned, build-ready tract called the Wright Business Park equipped with all city services fiber and WiFi. Festival Hydro invested $17 million to provide it with a redundant power station and grid upgrade. But still, they knew Stratford was a long shot to win the 400,000 square foot (37,000 sm2), C$400 million project.

> "The Stratford Principle" calls for the community to pioneer ICT-based solutions that are ultimately adopted across Canada.

Hopes were raised when Stratford was named to the short list. But then a team of site selectors from RBC came to town – like the president of CN before them – to break the bad news. Stratford was being disqualified because there was a wholesale natural gas depot unacceptably close to the planned location. Mayor Mathieson recalls asking if this was really the reason or just a rationale for a broader set of concerns. No, came the reply, it was the real reason. Mathieson spent the next couple of weeks working the phones until he got a commitment from the local manager of the gas company to move the depot to another location owned by the city – and for the bank to pay the cost. Stratford returned to the short list and emerged the eventual winner. Ground was broken in 2010 and the facility was operational by 2011.

Aside from the short-term construction jobs it brought, the data center is actually a small-time employer: fewer than 100 workers are onsite at any given time. But it validated Stratford's place in the digital economy – and the decision of companies like Scotiabank to retain their IT headquarters in the community. The third-largest bank in Canada, Scotiabank runs its global human resource functions and processes thousands of loan applications in multiple languages from its Stratford center, which IBM Canada uses as a test-bed in developing leading-edge systems that are deployed around the world.

The Stratford Principle

Stratford's leaders are determined that victories like the RBC data center turn out to be more than just the 21st Century version of chasing smoke-stacks. Stratford is pursuing a radical innovation agenda on two interlocking paths.

One is what Mathieson calls "The Stratford Principle." He wants to see his community lead in pioneering ICT-based solutions that are ultimately adopted across Canada. The city actively invites international companies to develop pilot applications using Stratford's high-quality broadband and electric infrastructure. Cisco works with Stratford and the Ontario government to pilot the use of its Telepresence videoconferencing technology to improve the delivery of services to constituents. A Virtual Concierge pilot has put Telepresence terminals into community centers, through which a city staffer can be "virtually present" to citizens in multiple locations. Ontario is funding a project to explore how the same technology can be use to give people with disabilities equal access to government services from their own homes.

A US-based company, Inter-Op, is using Stratford for its first Canadian deployment outside Toronto of an IP-based first-responder communications system. Emergency response around the world is hampered by incompatible systems purchased by different agencies that are unwilling to settle on a common standard. The Inter-Op platform makes it possible to connect different push-to-talk radios, telephones, mobile phones and satellite links on the same call, and to distribute images and video to those with computers, smartphones or tablets.

Toshiba is in Stratford testing how its LED lighting systems can be used to reduce the energy consumed by street lights. The Japanese company is there because of a trade mission by Stratford's leaders, in which Mayor Mathieson convinced Toshiba's chief technology officer to visit Stratford and see the benefits of piloting technology for North America in his small city. Toshiba also wants to learn from a small American company, anyCOMM, which has developed "intelligent lighting" technology. Retrofitted into street lighting, it can provide the same illumination at 5% of the power usage, but also makes each light in the network separately controllable using an embedded computer chip and

WiFi link. Using sustainable energy funding from the province, Stratford and anyCOMM have also developed a unique home automation program with Research in Motion and Festival Hydro. It will provide Stratford households with a subsidized package of anyCOMM intelligent light bulbs and a RIM Playbook that controls all of the bulbs remotely while linking to smart meters installed by Festival Hydro. The goal is to save power and reduce carbon emissions by giving residents a new level of control over energy use.

None of these represent successful business models yet. What they do represent is a high level of ambition – characteristic of Intelligent Communities – and skillful, cautious use of city resources. The partnerships leverage funding from the national and provincial government, and both money and expertise from corporations. The biggest resource that Stratford brings is not funding but vision, the attention of its leaders and the ability to coordinate multiple players in collaboration. As an official of the Canadian government put it, "When Stratford brings something to the table, it is serious."

Digital Media Economy

Stratford's other path leads to the media business of the future. The Festival, a major creator of intellectual property, gives the city a unique opportunity to create a digital media cluster that generates employment, new companies and a year-round source of prosperity.

Creating a cluster from the ground up, however, is challenging work. Stratford has gone about it with the same mix of high ambition, careful planning and the strategic use of outside resources.

A digital media cluster requires a highly-skilled population. Stratford sits at a center of a rural region that is losing population to larger cities and is challenged to afford the public education system it needs. With the support of the province, Stratford's school board has created an online high school called the Avon-Maitland e-Learning Center or AMDEC for short. It can provide a complete education for grades 9-12 through online text and interactive content, live chats, discussion boards and email. But most of its 1,200 student use it to supplement classroom learning. The availability of e-elearning ensures that every school in the district can offer a full and challenging curriculum while dealing with the rural reality that the physical footprint of schools must shrink to match the population. AMDEC also reaches out to drop-outs to help them earn credits and connect with employment opportunities.

In Stratford, two secondary schools offer specialized "high skills major" programs in digital media and information technology. In addition to learning such skills as videography and digital animation, the students engage in work-study with the Festival, where their talents find use both on stage and online, as well as with Rhyzome Networks and other employers.

In 2010, Stratford announced that the University of Waterloo would create a new campus in the community offering a Masters of Digital Experience Innovation. It took five years of work – involving three levels of government, local business leaders and the University – to bring it about. U Waterloo Stratford welcomed its first class in 2011. When both the graduate and undergraduate programs are fully operational, they will bring 500 students and about $43 million in new economic activity to the city.

The payoff for a digital media cluster is new companies. Stratford has attracted a commercialization center of the federally-funded Canadian Digital Media Network to the city. Mayor Mathieson has also persuaded the Greater Toronto AngelNet Investors (GTAN) to extend its reach to Stratford, where a GTAN-funded company, PowerNoodle, is already operation. PowerNoodle's cloud-based system helps organizations to collaborate online in brainstorming, prioritizing ideas and taking action. Another Stratford start-up, eJust Systems, provides a charge management system that lets police and public attorneys exchange arrest and charge data electronically, and which is already in use by one-quarter of the province's police forces.

Stratford is ready to see historical trends reverse themselves – for the brain drain to become a brain gain, as it builds industries including digital media, green energy, higher-value agriculture, and the precision manufacturing needed by transportation and aerospace. Its cultural strengths and lifestyle also equip it as a destination for "lone eagles," those high-skilled and entrepreneurial individuals who can work where they please so long as they have access to fast broadband. The latest cycle of reinvention will be underway for the next decade. But the elements in place today, and Stratford's record of adaptive, entrepreneurial leadership, suggest that success is within their grasp. ■

PLATFORMS FOR INNOVATION
More Lessons from Intelligent Communities

Leveraging University Innovation for Economic Growth
Dundee, Scotland, UK
Top7 Intelligent Community 2007, 2008, 2010

In 1991, the leaders of Dundee formed a collaborative body called the Dundee Partnership. Evolving from a project that focused on the physical regeneration of the city, the Partnership brought together all of the city's stakeholders: local and national government, business, education, the nonprofit sector and citizen leaders. Their mission was to forge a broader economic development vision for Dundee.

Early on, the Partnership commissioned research to identify economic strengths and weaknesses, gains and losses. As Dundee entered the 21st Century, the research uncovered the first net job growth in decades, despite a continuing fall in manufacturing employment and levels of unemployment higher than the national average. It was Dundee's university sector - including the University of Dundee, University of Abertay Dundee, the Ninewells teaching hospital and Scottish Crop Research Institute – that was creating jobs, not only in established sectors like publishing and scientific research, but in such new fields as software, animation, computer games, film and television.

The Partnership threw its energy into fanning the flames of entrepreneurship and accelerating the R&D that was the new engine of economic growth. Universities established graduate business incubators and policies promoting the spin-out of new companies. The University of Abertay Dundee opened the IC CAVE research center to support the computer game and digital entertainment sector. A Technopole located at the University of Dundee incubates science and technology start-ups that originate there.

A £20 million Digital Media Park entered into development and, by 2007, opened its first phase, consisting of 100,000 sq. feet (9290 m2) of space for e-businesses. A government-funded Business Gateway project began providing e-business training and support to small and mid-size companies, helping to improve the e-readiness of nearly 600 companies in 2004 and 2005. Two new marketing partnerships, bringing together public, private and academic leaders, launched Web sites, e-newsletters and conferences promoting "BioDundee" to attract life science companies and "Interactive Tayside" to the digital media sector. Interactive Tayside has 1,400 members from 380 companies, two of whom recently created a Digital Arts Festival called NEon to showcase technologies and local studios.

> No activity better represents Dundee's unique blend of ICT-driven innovation, education and marketing than 'Dare to Be Digital.'

Like an engine firing on all cylinders, the structured and institutionalized collaboration among Dundee sectors has driven forward the economy. The City Council's Web site began offering online payment and processing to the public in 2002. It provides more than 60 online applications, which generated 60,000 transactions and more than £8 million in fees and taxes in 2006.

Behind this online "front end," Dundee's IT department manages a citizen relationship management system called the Citizen Account. It captures data on citizens, with their permission, and uses it to create a single record of the citizen's interaction with government, which is saving the Council £400,000 per year. It captures, for example, the citizen's use of the Dundee Discovery Card, which replaced 10 separate card-related services in the city, for everything from bus service and parking to social services and student accounts at Abertay University. One of the outstanding benefits of the Discovery Card, in the eyes of the City Council, is that it eliminates the social stigma attached to social services cards for low-income residents. So popular has it become - with 44,000 cards issued, used by 87% of 12-18 year olds for school meals and bus travel, and 85% of +60 year olds for leisure access and bus travel - that the Scottish Government decided to deploy a multi-application card for the whole country and asked Dundee to run the program.

Probably no single activity better represents Dundee's unique blend of ICT-driven innovation, education and marketing savvy than Dare to Be Digital. Founded by Abertay University, Dare to Be Digital is a contest for students from throughout the UK and, increasingly, around the world. They submit ideas and designs for new video games to the Dare to Be Digital contest. The finalists come to Dundee for 10 weeks of intensive development with Abertay instructors and games industry professionals, at the end of which they have a finished game that is unveiled to judges and the public at a festival. Dundonians of all ages attend to play the games and vote on their choice for best game. The judges present awards as well – but the real prize for contestants is exposure to leading game designers and investors who come to Dundee from throughout the UK for the festival. ■

Executing a Comprehensive Innovation Strategy
Eindhoven, Netherlands
Intelligent Community of the Year 2011

Eindhoven is the high-tech manufacturing center of the Netherlands. The centerpiece of its innovation strategy is a public-private partnership called Brainport Development (www.brainport.nl). Its members include employers, research institutes, the Chamber of Commerce, the SRE, leading universities and the governments of the region's three largest cities. A small professional staff meets regularly with stakeholders to identify their strengths, needs and objectives, and then looks for opportunities for them to collaborate on business, social or cultural goals. Any stakeholder of Brainport has the opportunity to create new initiatives or partner with other stakeholders. Their work is based on a strategic plan called Brainport Navigator 2013 (with a 2020 version in the works funded in part by the Dutch government). It calls for focusing on five key areas for development: life technologies, automotive, high-tech systems, design and food & nutrition.

It sounds simple enough, and little different from strategies and collaboration groups at work in cities and regions around the globe. It could even be derided as a "talking shop" in which endless meetings take the place of action. But that would be a mistake.

Take healthcare. The region already has about 825 businesses active in the health sector, which employ 17,000 people. To drive further growth, Brainport created a project called Brainport Health Innovation (BHI). Its goals are to foster increased well-being for the elderly and chronically ill, to reduce healthcare costs and increase productivity, and to do so while generating economic opportunities for the region.

The total cost of regional healthcare is forecast to rise from €17bn now to €25bn by 2020, in large part because of the need for 100,000 new healthcare workers to meet demand. BHI's conservative goal is to improve productivity by 1 percent per year, which would reduce demand for new personnel by 25,000 and save about €750 million. Meanwhile, BHI's work expects to generate 150 new companies employing at least 10,000 people. It is a conscious effort to reduce employment demand in one area in order to increase it in another, where the region as a whole can benefit more.

> Brainport seeks to improve healthcare productivity by 1% per year while creating 150 new companies employing 10,000 people.

The range of Brainport projects is extraordinarily wide. The Automotive Technology Center involves 125 organizations in collaborative projects that, from 2005 to 2008, generated €4.5m in new investment. The start-up of new high-tech systems and ICT companies is stimulated by incubators with names like Catalyst, Beta II and the Device Process Building.

Design Connection Brainport manages a wide range of projects in design and technology, in order to encourage the industrial design expertise that is as essential as information technology to all of the SRE's industrial clusters.

Paradigit is a systems integrator founded in a university dormitory that built a fast-growing business producing build-to-order PCs and name-brand systems. Through membership in Brainport, the company identified an opportunity that turned into a program called SKOOL. This program provides over 800 Dutch primary schools with a combination of hardware and software that vastly simplifies the integration of information technology into education. Students receive SKOOL laptops from Paradigit. When students start up the laptops for the first time, the systems connect to the SKOOL server, download all of the applications specified for that school and configure themselves. SKOOL provides remote management of all servers and PCs at its client schools, as well as an online interface for students and teachers to communicate and share content securely. So "bullet-proof" is the hardware and software that SKOOL's tech support group consists of just three people.

The Taskforce Technology, Education and Employment program (abbreviated TTOA in Dutch) focuses on promoting the interest of young people in engineering, attracting foreign knowledge workers, career counseling and lifelong learning. As the financial crisis of 2009-2011 gripped the region, TTOA funded research projects for more than 2,000 workers who faced layoffs in order to preserve their skills until the economy recovered. An additional €670,000 went to retraining personnel within businesses. A Dutch entrepreneur's organization identified Helmond, the SRE's second largest city, as offering the Netherland's best response to economic crisis.

TTOA also goes on the road to international career fairs in the US, Europe, Turkey, India and China to promote opportunities in the Eindhoven region. Its Expatguideholland.com Web site provides information and services to smooth the path of highly-skilled immigrants and their families.

Information and communications technologies are also brought to bear on creating a quality of life that attracts and retains the digitally literate. Digital City Eindhoven attracts a half-million visitors monthly to a Web-based social media tool that encourages residents to learn more about the region. A WMO Portal involves 20 organizations in answering resident questions on health care, social services and housing. Bestuuronline puts political meetings in the city of Eindhoven online, while Virtual Helmond involves residents of that city in decision-making about planning, building designs and street furniture.

An online game called SenseOfTheCity allows anyone with a GPS-equipped mobile phone to create a personal map of the city and identify what they like best and least. A 12-day festival called STRP, which attracts 225,000 visitors, features music, film, live performances, interactive art, light art and robotics. GLOW is another festival that celebrates Eindhoven's history as home to the Phillips lighting division. The center of the city of Eindhoven is transformed for 10 days into an open-air museum of design in light, much of it interactive, for 65,000 visitors. ■

THE TOP7 OF 2012
Taichung City, Taiwan
A Mechanical Kingdom leads in the digital age

■ ROBERT BELL, CO-FOUNDER, ICF

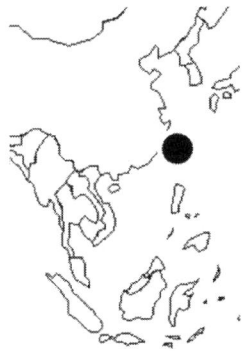

The roots of the city of Taichung City go back to 1897, when it was founded as the capital of what was then Taiwan Province. But in another sense, Taichung City was born on Christmas Day in 2010, when the modern city was merged with the surrounding county to create a municipality of 2.65 million people spread across 2,214 square kilometers (850 sq. mi.).

Much happened between those dates. In 1895, China ceded the island of Taiwan to Japan as spoils of the Sino-Japanese War. The Japanese administration created the surrounding Taichung County and invested in roads, dams and levees, and a north-south island railway project. Following the end of the Second World War, the city grew as a center of higher education, commerce and culture, where 70% of employees worked in service industries. The surrounding county developed manufacturing, which employed 48% of the workforce, and focused so successfully on precision machinery, from machine tools to bicycles, that it was nicknamed the "Mechanical Kingdom." But it also included remote mountain regions known for earthquakes, mud slides, avalanches and flooding, where the standard of living was a far cry from that of city dwellers.

Taichung City In Brief

Population
2,661,290

Labor Force
1,284,000

Size
2,215 km^2

Top Industries
Services, electro-optical, precision machinery, hand tools, bicycles, biotechnology.

Broadband Penetration
75% households, 99% business, 100% government, 100% education.

Degrees Awarded
Undergrad 13,478; graduate 4,613.

3-Year Job Creation
666,719 (36,050 net), 233,798 depending on ICT.

Key Leaders

Mayor Chih-Chiang (Jason) Hu

Kuo-Ching Chen, Vice General Manager, Chungwha Telecom, Southern Taiwan Business

Chuang-Chun Chiu, Vee Telecom Multimedia

Chen-Huan Tang, General Director, Service Systems Tech Center, Industrial Tech Research Institute

---

Those disparities – between service and manufacturing, urban and rural – were a challenge to the very idea of the merger, which sought to create a metropolitan area ready for global competition. The new Taichung certainly had the potential. It was the only city on the island at the intersection of four transport systems: seaport, airport, rail and road. Under its dynamic Mayor, Chih-Chiang (Jason) Hu, the city leadership set out to realize the potential they saw in Taichung – a potential that could only be realized if all the economic, social and cultural pieces of the jigsaw puzzle fit snugly into place.

Lightpaths and Airwaves

As Taiwan's third-largest city, Taichung benefits from the presence of two competing broadband carriers: the national incumbent Chungwha Telecom and Vee Telecom Multimedia, an aggressive young company that is deploying 4G WiMAX wireless services in Taichung and nationwide.

Chungwha has a goal, set by the national government's M Taiwan Project, to provide 100 Mbps service to six million users across Taiwan by 2015. Working in collaboration with city government, Chungwha has grown its optical fiber coverage from 40% of the metro area in 2010 to 94% in 2012. Eighty-five percent of companies in Taichung's many industrial parks are customers, and nearly 95% of all Chungwha fiber customers have access to a minimum of 10 Mbps, with 50 Mbps available to almost 80%. Taichung's government expects the city to be the first in Taiwan to offer 100 Mbps fiber service throughout its service area.

Vee Telecom has boosted coverage of its wireless network from 70% before the merger to 91%. With prices as low as US$20 per month, the company has achieved high customer satisfaction rates of more than 90%. Vee Telecom plays a vital role in extending the high-speed network cost-effectively to the more remote, mountainous areas of Taichung, as well as ensuring access to broadband for citizens on the move. The company also collaborates with the city on special projects. It has installed touch-screen mobile Internet terminals in taxis and buses to provide local real-time information to passengers on everything from traffic conditions to cultural and entertainment offerings. It is also pioneering in IPTV over 4G and providing customers across Taichung with a television that can access not only conventional programming but also Facebook, YouTube and online educational offerings using a remote control.

The city is a major customer for both companies, because its leaders view this high-quality connectivity as the key to uniting the vast metropolis. The merger created the opportunity to make once-in-a-generation changes to the way government organizes itself and delivers service to citizens, and Taichung is using information and communications technology to drive the change.

As more than 150 city and county agencies were consolidated and reorganized, it became a major challenge to reflect these changes online. But the new consolidated city Web site, launched on Christmas 2010, proved a hit. Site visits exceeded 5 million within a few days and grew four times in the next nine months. Taichung's government also created a single service platform for public service and consumer inquiries, and introduced a 24/7 hotline that offered counseling services, assistance with inquiries and applications, non-emergency reporting and emergency dispatch.

ICT for Safety and Security

Rapid population growth in the city and county had led over the years to an uncomfortably high crime rate. The New Taichung City Police Bureau began planning in 2007 to use information and communications technology to secure the much larger area that would soon be its responsibility. The Bureau expanded its network of surveillance cameras to more than 11,000 and created a Web-based digital recording system for data capture. It launched a central mission command system and a GPS-based license plate recognition system able to capture and match 90% of license plates. These systems contributed to resolving nearly 7,000 cases through February 2012.

Taichung's government also developed an intelligent traffic management system that uses almost 100 surveillance cameras and nearly 500 GPRS-controlled traffic signals to monitor and manage traffic flow, improving safety and reducing travel time and pollution. The fixed network is supplemented by a vehicle-based set of cameras to target trouble spots. Data from the system is available to residents through a GIS application that enables smartphone users to both view and contribute traffic information.

> Taichung is home to 13 universities, many of them located in science parks where research institutes and leading-edge businesses congregate.

To increase the use of mass transit, the city worked with local bus companies to install hundreds of "smart bus stops" with LED displays showing the estimated arrival time of the next bus. Buses are equipped with GPS tracking systems that feed the network as well their own onboard display and announcement system that identifies the next step and estimated time of arrival in multiple languages. The major bus line, Taichung Transit Jet, began offering an 8-km free ride promotion in 2011 to encourage use of public transportation, and saw passenger rides triple to 4.6 million from 2007 to 2011, saving an estimated one million tons of greenhouse gases.

The University-Business Connection

Taichung is home to 13 universities, many of them located in science parks where research institutes and leading-edge businesses congregate. The largest is Feng Chia University with 21,000 students, followed by Tunghai University with 17,000 and Chung Hsing University with 16,000. Feng Chai alone has launched more than 40 research institutes, which it seeks to fund entirely through private-sector projects and government contracts. Its 15-year-old GIS Institute has over 150 full-time staff as well as interns and students involved in developing digital mapping, remote sensors, robot vehicles and flying drones to monitor severe weather and changes to the Earth.

Altogether, Taichung's universities house 13 incubation centers focusing on everything from digital technology and biotechnology to plastics, footwear and recreation services. Connecting them is the Taichung Incubators Business Alliance, which aims to nurture the growth of the more than 400 businesses that operate from the incubators. The city also facilitated the development of Taiwan's only Academia-Industry Training Alliance, which aims to sharpen the skills of both established and new businesses. The Alliance offers training courses in precision machinery, machine tools, mechanical and electrical control and photovoltaic systems. More than 120 manufacturers have sent 800 employees to Alliance Courses since 2006.

Taichung's industrial parks play a key role in economic growth. The Central Taiwan Science Park opened in 2003 and has attracted companies in solar energy, touch-panel displays, optoelectronics, precision chemicals, semiconductors equipment, aerospace and ICT. In 2011, those companies had combined revenues exceeding US$8 billion. Nine other parks at various phases of development, including the Precision Machinery Technology Park, are expected to generate 60,000 new jobs.

Major success stories include Taiwan Semiconductor Manufacturing Company, which broke ground in 2010 for its 15th silicon wafer "fab" at the Central Taiwan Science Park. With the ability to produce nanometer-scale components on 12-inch silicon wafers, it represents a US$10 billion investment and total employment of 8,000 workers. Hon Hai Technology Group has invested US$3.3 billion in developing R&D and manufacturing facilities for precision machinery. AU Optronics Corporation manufactures large LCD displays and solar panels. The US$12.7 billion company has 43,000 employees around the world. But not everything in Taichung is high-tech. The Giant Manufacturing Company was founded in 1972 by eight people with a passion for bicycle design and manufacturing. Over the past 40 years, it has become a global icon of excellence that is the first choice of international cycling teams. Forbes magazine named it one of the world's "200 Best Small Companies" for four consecutive years.

Inside the i-Park

Taiwan's national government has an "i-Park" strategy for the country's vast number of science and industrial parks, backed by substantial financial incentives for research and development. It encourages the parks to use information and communications technology to create applications that improve quality of life, to master key technologies and to scale their operations for global markets.

Taichung has applied the i-Park concept to its precision manufacturing cluster. At the Taichung Precision Machinery Technology Park, Taichung Industrial Park and other facilities, more than 400 manufacturers use a shared Engineering Data Bank Service developed by Taichung's Industrial Technology Research Institute. The Data Bank aims to overcome a challenge faced by small-to-midsize manufacturers: the stratospheric cost of IT systems to manage product design, enterprise resource planning and customer service. A secure cloud-based platform, the Data Bank offers these capabilities on a cost-effective, shared-use basis, and companies using it have seen a 16% reduction in R&D time-to-market and gains of 18% in process efficiency.

> Taichung residents have long been open to other cultures and willing to experiment with what they have to offer.

Under the i-Park banner, the Research Institute has also launched a collaborative program to reduce the energy consumption of manufacturers by deploying advanced hardware and software and implementing process improvements. The resulting gains in efficiency contribute to the companies' bottom lines as well as Taichung's environmental goals.

Taichung Harbor has massive container truck traffic in and out of the port, which requires secure handling and verification. Until 2011, that meant unloading and physically checking cargo, creating a bottleneck that hurt the port's competitiveness and added to air pollution. In 2011, Taichung Harbor launched an automatic gate checkpoint system that electronically reads and matches the truck driver's identification, license plate numbers and container numbers using RFID technology. The entire process now takes 2-3 minutes, and the automatic verification has proven almost 99% accurate.

Competitive Advantage

Perhaps because they live in a port city, Taichung residents have long been open to other cultures and willing to experiment with what they have to offer. The city was the first in Taiwan to develop Western-style restaurants and the British tradition of afternoon tea. This taste for culture has accelerated in the age of globalization. In 2009, residents took part in an average of 35 arts and cultural events per person, compared with 4 events per person in 2001. In that same year, Taichung opened the Taichung Cultural & Creative Industries Park, built on the foundations of an old winery, to the public.

Since 1996, Taichung has held the Da Dun Fine Art Competition, which has attracted 12,500 artists from around the world – including Pavarotti, Jose Carreras, Yo-Yo Ma and Lady Gaga – to present their works at its grand festival. Art galleries and a science museum, botanical gardens and a string of parks, dot the urban landscape.

Arts, culture and overall quality of life are important contributors to Taichung's success in the broadband economy. They create the environment that attracts and retains innovative individuals and companies. So do Taichung's "Fair Digital Opportunities" programs, which connect elderly and low-income residents, as well as those living in remote areas, to digital skills. Three Digital Opportunity Training Centers offer more than 100 courses in digital literacy and life and work skills, as well as projects that seek to promote local culture online. Taichung also taps national government funding to provide low-income children with free computers and subsidized connection to the city's high-speed broadband. Free Internet access is available at over 300 locations in the city, from libraries to cultural centers and government offices.

In 2007 Taichung introduced an online reading certification program for elementary and middle school children. The system allows teachers to establish an online book database and assessment library. Students read books at varying levels, both in school and at home, and take an online comprehension test. A passing grade gets them a printable certificate. Dedicated teachers have posted nearly 10,000 books to the system, and students have received 5.5 million certificates. The system helps students build strong reading habits while incorporating digital literacy into the curriculum.

Under Taiwan's President Ying-Jeou Ma, the nation has committed itself to become an Intelligent Island – an idea he developed while serving as Mayor of Taipei, ICF's 2006 Intelligent Community of the Year. President Ma is also responsible for significantly improving ties with mainland China and deepening a trade relationship that is already worth US$110 billion per year. A cross-Strait trade signed in 2010 is expected to boost Taiwan's annual GDP by a further 4-5%. With its world-class industrial parks, high-tech transportation, innovative companies and globally-connected citizens, the Mechanical Kingdom is clearly ready to play its part and reap the gains. ■

CONCLUSION
The Path Forward

■ LOUIS ZACHARILLA, CO-FOUNDER, ICF

It is an ugly thing to watch a once-great community fading away and about to die.

Most die slowly. Like a species long endangered and unable to thrive in the crush of an overwhelming economic evolution, they simply lose relevance over a time. Their hope for anything better is reduced to a distant memory of glory days. All seems lost. Crime grows, schools get worse, jobs run away, downtowns turn dark and kids pack and become adults elsewhere. They simply hang on and, in the words of Pink Floyd, live in "quiet desperation." It is painful to be in such a place and hard to witness one.

We are now in an era where many communities around the world are simply hanging on. Some have withered and for all practical purposes surrendered, while others have for all practical purposes perished. Only the smokestacks, unused and crumbling, remain visible. The consequences of this erosion can be seen, felt and even heard. *National Geographic* reported, in July 2012, that one language dies every 14 days. If this continues we can expect that, by the turn of the next century, as many as half of the 7,000 languages spoken on this Earth will have disappeared as communities abandon native tongues in favor of more economically convenient ones. When a language is lost, a culture and way of life go with it.

Faced with this all-but-inevitable decline, someone somewhere first said "no more." No more decay. We do not know when or where that first defiant voice was raised. But we do know, from the seven stories we have told you here, that a community's desire to persist, its demand to thrive, are among its greatest assets. They are what give rise to courage and defiance. The belief that a place is worth saving – that a home town may still contain the oxygen the human spirit needs to breathe – eventually turns into policies and programs. New types of leaders emerge. Ideas flourish. Soon, collaboration and planning begin to unearth the investments of the past and give them new purpose. As the Top7 have done, they rediscover what made them a community in the first place and what makes them special today. This happens again and again, paying dividends by way of job creation, social capital, cultural richness and that quality beyond all qualities necessary for human persistence: hope.

Success is an infection. It spreads. To quote the poet, Virgil, "They can because they think they can."

The Top7 Intelligent Communities of the Year give us all hope. They defy what some say is the demographic and migratory destiny of human beings at this time in history. Place is irrelevant, they say. Only enormous places are where it's at. Home is not nearly so important any more.

They are wrong. This is true neither for a big city or a small one. Some places, like Stratford, tell us that the small-town attitude is capable of earning the same rewards as larger places. As its Mayor, Dan Mathieson, told business leaders during a memorable January 2012 speech in North Canton, Ohio, "We are going to show those big cities that they don't have it all. That we small cities have a place and a future along with them."

This language of battle – a fight finely armed by the arsenal of broadband and increasingly layered with the applications of knowledge and innovation – is being heard in the more than 100 Intelligent Communities of all shapes and sizes around the world. Their noise is no longer an act of desperation but a song of a modern renaissance.

In Riverside the mayor, a thoughtful, forceful and determined gentleman, made it his priority to refurbish a long-neglected graveyard where the city's founder was buried and forgotten. Not long after, he walked the red carpet to our awards ceremony and found himself accepting, on behalf of his city, the Intelligent Community of the Year Award. The social media response from his citizens, many of whom had returned from other places to save it, zinged across the Web. "We are so proud," they wrote. "We earned it," they tweeted. "I love my city," they posted. These are the words of warriors who know the price and the reward of the struggle to find a place they can call home.

There are many ways to draw the battle lines and many different feints an enemy can throw at a place to keep it from becoming intelligent. Saint John had the largest per-capita decline in manufacturing over a four-year period of any place in Canada. Oulu, seemingly marooned in its isolation not far from the icy Arctic, watched its biggest company slip and fall. Taichung City was choking on greenhouse gases and struggling to turn a vast region into a unified city. But each overcame the challenge thrown at it and struck back. The beautiful Image Mill in Quebec City (Le Moulin à images) today tells the city's story on a projection screen 600 meters long and 30 meters high, mounted on the side of silos filled with grain. The city's past and future meet there, and the pride and creativity overflow with the noise of a place where a heritage of culture and creativity has become an export industry and an economic enabler.

Where do seven communities as diverse and geographically distant as the Top7 of 2012 go from here?

If language is any guide, the names of the projects they have launched provide a poetic clue. There is "Quebec Seeks Solutions." There is "Project Bridge" and "True Growth" and a "PanOULU Network." There is the capstone phrase that our international jury said could stand for our entire movement: Riverside's "Seizing Our Destiny." That is what they have all done. It is a path every community can follow. Seizing destiny is what every politician, academic institution, business and citizen must do. The challenge is to make it work economically, socially and emotionally. It is a holistic requirement. It demands to be sustained.

During a visit to Suwon, Korea, the Intelligent Community of the Year in 2010, I learned something new about Buddhism. In that faith tradition, there is a confusing answer to a common question: "What does enlightenment feel like?" The answer is that it is a state where one "is neither advancing, nor retreating, nor standing still."

The Top7 face a similar question and each must find its own answer. Having been named to the Top7, or as Intelligent Community of the Year, do they advance? Do they retreat? Do they stand still?

It is all of the above. They may slow down to allow the community to understand what going forward means. They may take time to learn from their peer communities. The Intelligent Community Awards are both a call to reflect and a call to never stop advancing. The Top7 have been weighed among the leading communities of the world, and have been found to be leaders. But the only criteria that really counts is what a citizen of that community says at the end of a day of good work – coming home, looking around and saying "I am glad that I live here. I love this place."

For the Top7, many of whom experienced nothing but decline for so long, arriving on the world's stage was an awakening. The first reaction was disbelief. This turned, slowly, into an embrace of what and where they were at this moment in time. A new voice could be heard in coffee shops, classrooms and City Hall. An old language was revived. The town center lit again – often with the latest generation of energy-saving lamps – and the sense of disbelief became a claim and a call to action. That call is from more and more citizens who say that, despite that "award we got in New York," their community is not done yet. It is not even close to where it can be. There is more work to do.

The right thing to do, if the rest of the communities in the world are wise, is to embrace the sound of that beautiful noise. ■

Appendix

The Intelligent Community Indicators

In a study funded by the Province of Ontario, Canada, the Intelligent Community Forum defined five critical success factors for the creation of Intelligent Communities. This list of Intelligent Community Indicators, as the study termed them, provided the first conceptual framework for understanding all of the factors that determine a community's competitiveness in the Broadband Economy. In its work since then, ICF has also identified a number of success factors for Intelligent Communities in both industrialized and developing nations.

1. **Broadband Connectivity**

    Broadband is the new essential utility, as vital to economic growth as clean water and good roads. Intelligent Communities express a clear vision of their broadband future and craft policies to encourage deployment and adoption.

2. **Knowledge Workforce**

    A knowledge workforce is a labor force that creates economic value through the acquisition, processing and use of information. Intelligent Communities exhibit the determination and demonstrated ability to develop a workforce qualified to perform knowledge work from the factory floor to the research lab and from the construction site to the call center or Web design studio.

3. Digital Inclusion

As broadband deploys widely through a community, there is serious risk that it will worsen the exclusion of people who already play a peripheral role in the economy and society, whether due to poverty, lack of skills, prejudice or geography. Intelligent Communities promote digital inclusion by creating policies and funding programs that provide "have-nots" with access to digital technology and broadband, by providing skills training and by promoting a compelling vision of the benefits that the broadband economy.

4. Innovation

For business, broadband has become to innovation what fertilizer is to crops. Intelligent Communities work to build the local innovation capacity of new companies, because these produce all of the job growth in modern economies, and invest in e-government programs that reduce their costs while delivering services on the any-where-anytime basis that digitally savvy citizens expect.

5. Marketing and Advocacy

Like businesses facing greater global competition, communities must work harder than ever to communicate their advantages and explain how they are maintaining or improving their position as wonderful places to live, work and build a growth business. Effective marketing shares this story with the world, while advocacy builds a new vision of the community from within.

The Intelligent Community Indicators provide communities with a frame-work for assessment, planning and development, as they work to build prosperous local economies in the Broadband Economy. The Indicators also reveal the interactions that can create a "virtuous cycle" of positive change. Broadband connectivity feeds the development of a knowledge workforce as well as creating the foundation of digital inclusion programs. Both contribute to a rising level of innovation in the community as well as increasing demand for connectivity. And Intelligent Communities make this wave of change the core "value proposition" in economic development marketing.

In its annual Awards program, ICF includes as a sixth criteria a theme that changes from year to year but focuses on a particular success factor in the development of Intelligent Communities. This white paper has been devoted to exploring the annual theme. ICF asks communities completing the Intelligent Community Award nomination forms are asked to provide specific information on their efforts and successes in this area. ∎

The Broadband Economy

Whether you know it or not, you are living in the Broadband Economy. It is the new global economy – what many call "globalization" – emerging from the deployment of broadband around the planet.

It is an economy in which, for all intents and purposes, the hard-working people of Mumbai, Shenzen and Bangladesh live right next door to the hard-working people of Montreal, San Francisco and Berlin, because their communities are connected. It is an economy based on digital collaboration and cooperation across time zones and cultures, which has opened markets, boosted productivity, created employment, and improved living standards. In the Broadband Economy, companies look for opportunities to locate their facilities where they can gain the greatest advantage in terms of cost, skills and access to markets. So does money: broadband has made capital investment in businesses, factories and facilities highly mobile. Billions of US dollars move around the globe daily in pursuit of a competitive return on investment, and when trouble strikes a nation's economy, that mobile capital can flee at devastating speed.

But while global business may be mobile, communities are not. Communities everywhere have the same goal: to be a place where people can raise their children and give those young people enough economic opportunity to allow them to stay and raise children of their own. In the Broadband Economy, that task is more challenging than ever. Where geographic location and natural resources were once the key determiners of a community's economic potential, it is increasingly the skills of the labor force, and the ability of business and government to adapt and innovate, that power job creation.

The Broadband Economy may challenge communities, but it also hands them powerful new tools to build competitive and inclusive economies. Broadband offers smaller communities in remote locations the opportunity to move from the periphery to the center in economic terms. It enables small companies to be global exporters - including the export of skills and knowledge which were never before transportable across time zones or national borders. It can ensure that schools in remote regions have access to the latest information tools and reference sources. It can link healthcare providers to leading medical centers and local law enforcement to national information grids. By boosting the economic and social well-being of communities, it can reduce the incentives for their young people to move away in search of opportunity and a better quality of life. Paradoxically, it can play a key role in giving communities a sustainable future in our ever-more-connected world. ∎

Notes

[1] *Innovation Nation*, John Kao, Free Press, 2007, pages 188-189

[2] *A Legal Bridge Spanning 100 Years: From the Gold Mines of El Dorado to the 'Golden' Startups of Silicon Valley* by Gregory Gromov 2010.

[3] "Wired world - the global growth of mobile phone use" by Paddy Allen, *The Guardian*, March 2, 2009.

[4] *Cisco Visual Networking Index: Global Mobile Data Traffic Forecast Update, 2010–2015*, February 1, 2011.

[5] Intelligent Community profile of Chattanooga, Tennessee, USA at www.intelligentcommunity.org.

[6] *Management: Tasks, Responsibilities, Practices* by Peter F. Drucker, Harper & Row, 1973.

[7] Richard Maulsby, director of public affairs for the U.S. Patent & Trademark Office, quoted in Karen E. Klein, Smart Answers, "Avoiding the Inventor's Lament," *BusinessWeek*, November 10, 2005.

[8] "Where Innovation Creates Value" by Amar Bhide, *McKinsey Quarterly*, February 2009.

Made in the USA
Charleston, SC
23 March 2014